CHILDREN OF THE
NEW MILLENNIUM

OTHER BOOKS BY P. M. H. ATWATER

I Died Three Times in 1977

The Frost Diamond

Life Sounds

Brain Shift/Spirit Shift: A Theoretical Model Using Research on Near-Death States to Explore the Transformation of Consciousness

Coming Back to Life

The Magical Language of Runes

Beyond the Light

Future Memory

Goddess Runes

CHILDREN
OF THE NEW
MILLENNIUM

Children's Near-Death
Experiences and the
Evolution of Humankind

P.M.H. ATWATER, Lh.D.

THREE RIVERS PRESS

New York

Published by Three Rivers Press
201 East 50th Street, New York, New York 10022.
Member of the Crown Publishing Group.
Random House, Inc. New York, Toronto, London, Sydney, Auckland
www.randomhouse.com
THREE RIVERS PRESS is a registered trademark of
Random House, Inc.
Printed in the United States of America
Design by Susan Hood

Library of Congress Cataloging-in-Publication Data
Atwater, P. M. H.
Children of the new millennium : children's near-death experiences
and the evolution of humankind / by P. M. H. Atwater. — 1st pbk. ed.
Includes bibliographical references and index.
1. Near-death experiences in children.   2. Human evolution—
Miscellanea.   I. Title.
BF1045.N42A88   1999
133.9—dc21   99-25229
                                                            CIP

ISBN 0-609-80309-3
10 9 8 7 6 5 4 3 2 1
First Edition

It is with the deepest love and affection that I dedicate this book to Kenneth L. Johnston, my father, a man considered by most who know him to be one of the finest police officers ever to have worn a badge. I grew up immersed in police work thanks to him; the police station in Twin Falls, Idaho, my second home. Life extremes were daily fare then, and my father's insistence that I learn the techniques of investigative fieldwork later evolved into the research protocol I came to use in my explorations of the near-death phenomenon. I call myself the "gumshoe of near-death" because of this, and I am forever grateful to my father for his teachings and his love.

ACKNOWLEDGMENTS

My sincerest gratitude goes to the 277 people who participated in this study of child experiencers of near-death states. Although many were youngsters when I interviewed them, the rest had reached their teen years or were in varying stages of adulthood. All of them bared their souls and shared their secrets about what it is *really* like to experience the near-death phenomenon as a child. I am awestruck by their courage in being so open and humbled at their willingness to trust me with their joy and their pain.

Those who provided extra support are listed below. As is true of any endeavor of this magnitude, it is impossible to name everyone. So, to each and all, I give my deepest thanks!

Terry Young Atwater
Stephany Evans
William G. Reimer
Melvin Morse
Diane K. Corcoran
Theresa A. Csanady

Acknowledgments

Todd Murphy
Leslie Dixon
Joseph Benedict Geraci
Pat Kennedy
Donald Riggs
Andrew Swyschuk
L. Suzanne Gordon
Alejandra Warden
Sarah Hinze
Mellen-Thomas Benedict
Kelly John Huffman
Natalie Rowell
Paulie Coiner
Dennis Swartz

CONTENTS

FLY

To think that i could
*   FLY, like you,*
above this complicated place
*   to know that it is*
*   i, untrue,*
is something i can't seem to face
*   at all. To feel that*
*   sun, like you,*
upon my cotton candy back . . .
*   aware that i am*
*   one who flew*
so long ago, i cry and rack
*   my brain for one faint*
*   memory*
of freedom high above the earth,
*   of FLYING . . . but i*
*   cannot see.*
'Twas way before my second birth.

Janet Blessing, Pittsfield, Massachusetts. Her
near-death experience occurred at nine months
of age during a bout of pneumonia. She wrote
this poem when she was nineteen.

FOREWORD

It may be that the greatest value of a book is its ability to disturb, unless one wants only to be entertained. In either case, *Children of the New Millennium* is quite a cup of tea. This heady adventure into the inner world just may be P. M. H. Atwater's magnum opus, though it can become threatening and disturbing to our commonly held assumptions. (At least it was to mine.)

Read with an unprejudiced eye, or mind (which, again, was not easy for me), it surely should rank with William James's classic *The Varieties of Religious Experience,* if nothing else. Like James's work, it raises a rich substrate of unanswered questions concerning the nature of the human mind and its incomparable, awesome creativity. Thus this is a seminal work, demanding further and deep philosophical inquiry and objective pursuit, while at the same time a work of astonishing thoroughness, brilliance, insight, and prodigious admirable research.

Atwater has simply covered her subject with impeccable thoroughness, even as her rigorously disciplined approach opens her subject to a wider question that might be beyond the scope of any single book. And she wisely knows when to leave a question hanging (always risky academically), rather than trying to make the definitive statement about *everything,* as some of us are wont to do. Every time I think she has boxed herself into an untenable position, she offers counterexperiences that prove to be outside that box and that show her objectivity toward any part of the remarkably rich material she has gathered. And much of this material is academically suspect—politically incorrect, so to speak—even as it is undeniably a rich segment of actual human experience, material that resonates with my own history as it will with that of many readers (whereas the academically/politically correct tends to leave *me* as a lived experience rather out of the picture).

Surely there are unresolved issues in this book, as there would have to be in a work of this scope. Time and again I wanted to stop and insist on battling out some issue, though it might take years. Memory itself is a gaping black hole of mystery, in spite of all the research into this area. False memory has been the subject of much study. Shared, archetypal memory is almost surely a real phenomenon. Nobelist Gerald Edelman claims that memory is quite organic, shifting, growing, changing, the brain-mind continually updating and reshuffling its memory. Contrary to current academic opinion, David Chamberlain denies that memory is "in the brain" at all, and gives serious evidence to back his point. I just received a disturbing paper concerning our "biomythological memory" that remakes itself continually on behalf of rationalization, self-aggrandizement, apology, and what Caroline Myss calls "woundology." Atwater's contribution to this perplexing and open-ended issue should prove rich and ongoing. I trust this book will be read and accepted by a wide population.

Joseph Chilton Pearce
July 31, 1998

PREFACE

Only those who have dared to let go can dare to reenter.

Meister Eckhart

Twenty years ago I died, not once but three times within a span of three months. The year was 1977. A miscarriage and extreme hemorrhaging started it all, followed by a major thrombosis in the right-thigh vein that dislodged and the worst case of phlebitis the specialist had ever heard of, let alone seen. These events happened on January 2 and January 4, respectively. Three months later I suffered a physical, mental, and emotional collapse. Doctors were seen after the fact, so no one was in actual attendance when I died, yet it is the opinion of a gynecologist that I did indeed die, and that is my opinion also.

Regaining full use of my body and my faculties proved to be a daunting task, made more difficult by three relapses in September and October, one of which was adrenal failure. My blood pressure reading at that time was sixty over sixty. For me, coming back from death meant relearning how to crawl, stand, walk, run, climb stairs, tell the difference between left and right, and see and hear properly. It also meant redefining and rebuilding my belief systems.

The specter of insanity became the greater challenge, though, as dealing with three different near-death episodes demanded more from me than dying ever had. I was absolutely overwhelmed by the experience *and* its after-effects. My previous background in the paranormal and altered states of consciousness was of little help. Dreams and visions offered no solace. For a while, I was lost between worlds, belonging to none of them.

What I dealt with in reidentifying myself and my place in the human family is described in chapter 2 of my first book, *Coming Back to Life: The After-Effects of the Near-Death Experience,*[1] and chapters 11, 13, and 15 in *Future Memory: How Those Who "See the Future" Shed New Light on the Workings of the Human Mind.*[2] Although bits and pieces of my personal story have been inserted into every book I have ever written, my primary work, first and foremost, is *research.* Why? Because it's my job.

Let me explain.

During my third near-death experience, I reached what I believe to be the Centerpoint of Existence. Many revelations were given to me while there—about creation and consciousness and the journey of the soul. Afterward, a voice spoke. I came to regard it as the Voice Like None Other, for it was all-powerful, all-knowing, everywhere present, and of God. The Voice said: "Test revelation. You are to do the research. One book for each death." Books two and three were named, but not book one. I was shown what each book was to contain, but not how to proceed or what such a project might entail. I accepted the assignment.

My research of the near-death phenomenon began in earnest once I was back in my body and had sufficiently recovered from the trauma of my deaths, and had left my home state of Idaho and zigzagged across the continent to the Old Dominion of Virginia. It was mid-November 1978, and I had work to do. Immediately, I set about doing it.

For more than twenty years, with only what monies I could scrape together, I have quietly moved among a special populace, those who had, like me, survived their deaths—asking questions and observing ever so intently the *behavior* of those who answered, as well as that of their families, friends, and caregivers. I learned through hard experience how to speak in "sound bites" once the media discovered I existed, but, fortunately, any fame I tasted was fleeting enough to allow me the time I needed to investigate the field of near-death states and consciousness transformations from 360 degrees . . . what was *really* there, whether or not it was what I wanted or expected to see. I was able to look through the eyes of over three thousand near-death survivors—a figure that doubles in number if you count the people I worked with and interviewed back in the sixties and early seventies when I was actively involved in exploring "otherworld journeys." (My work in the sixties led me to initiate Idaho's first nonprofit metaphysical corporation dedicated to an objective examination of mysticism and spiritual awakenings. Headquartered in Boise, Inner Forum existed for six years under my tutelage and one year under the direction of a board of directors, before it was replaced by the Creative Living Institute.)

Like other experiencers in the annals of near-death studies, I was shown my mission. Researching the near-death phenomenon and what it implies is why I returned from death. In my books, I pass along to others clear and tested material that provides a context for further inquiry and lends perspective to intriguing but elusive mysteries—about the mind, and about life and death.

I also do what I do because it's my passion, because, as the great paleontologist and Jesuit scholar Pierre Teilhard de Chardin once said, "Research is the highest form of adoration."

I came to know God in death . . . and I haven't stopped celebrating since.

My whole life is an aftereffect.

John Raymond Liona, Brooklyn, New York.
His near-death experience occurred during birth trauma.

CHILDREN OF THE
NEW MILLENNIUM

ONE

EVOLUTION'S NOD

The test of a first-rate intelligence is the ability to hold two opposed ideas in the mind at the same time, and still retain the ability to function.

F. Scott Fitzgerald

Children of the new millennium are different from those of any other generation of record. They are unusually smart, even gifted; identify with "alien" existences whether past-life oriented, extraterrestrial, or multidimensional; and they are natural creative intuitives.

William Strauss and Neil Howe, authors of *Generations: The History of America's Future, 1584 to 2069,*[1] label the children born between 1982 and about 2003 as our nation's fourteenth, or "millennial," generation. These youngsters are arriving at a time in our history when countless measures for the protection of the young are being swept into law. They are turning out to be the most wanted, the most nurtured, the most educated, the most dedicated to public service, ever.

And this is true globally.

Millennial children are not confined to the boundaries of any one country, as this observation from Ibarra Chavez, a

Mexican pediatrician, proves: "The new crop of infants are coming in more *aware* . . . eyes focused and alert, necks strong, lying in bassinets no bigger than chickens, and with a *knowingness* I cannot describe [in Spanish or in English]. They are very special babies, this new crop."

Sharon Begley, author of the *Newsweek* magazine article entitled "The IQ Puzzle,"[2] describes the situation this way: "IQ scores throughout the developed world have soared dramatically since the tests were introduced in the early years of this century. . . . The rise is so sharp that it implies that the average school child today is as bright as the near-geniuses of yesteryear."

The gene pool cannot change fast enough to account for this jump. So it has been supposed that better nutrition and more efficient schools are the cause. Yet neither factor explains the fascinating incongruity that appeared in IQ test scores: acquired intelligence, which comes from rote schooling, improved only slightly, while nonverbal intelligence, which is based on creative problem solving, soared!

Trying to make sense of this, experts have surmised that either kids are getting better at taking tests, or something in their environment accounts for this astonishing difference. Some top educators feel that the spread of image-intense technologies, like video games, for example, are probably at least partially responsible since they train a child to concentrate and respond—major components to learning (unlike regular television, which demands nothing of viewers). Other professionals suggest that it may be permissive or relaxed parenting, which results in the child leading the parent, that can promote the critical skill of vocabulary building.

Whatever the cause, the global jump in youngsters' intelligence amounts to about a 24- to 26-point rise over the IQ score used during the first half of this century as a marker for genius, at around 134. This directly challenges the entire academic understanding of what constitutes genius and how it is measured.

Surprisingly, the research of near-death states I have conducted since 1978 shows that roughly half of those children who have experienced the near-death phenomenon fall within this same score range, upward to 150, 160, and even higher. But their jump in intelligence was *sudden* and could be traced to that moment when death seemed their only option—not playing with video games or trying to outwit parents. They were not born that way. And few of those I interviewed ever used image-intense technologies; the majority described parental bonding as "strained." Although the end result of their experience matches the changes currently being observed with millennial kids, how they got that way differs radically.

The incongruity in test scores, though, concerns nonverbal intelligence or creative problem solving. *Nearly all of the child experiencers in my twenty-plus years of researching near-death states came to exhibit this trait* (genius or not), *followed by a noticeable decrease for most of them in the ability to express themselves and socialize.*

Commonalities between the millennial generation and child experiencers of near-death episodes are so numerous (nonverbal intelligence being just one) that to understand what might be happening with the new crop of young people worldwide, we would be wise to take a closer look at the near-death experience *and* its aftereffects—at how children are *really* affected by the phenomenon of experiencing life *after* death.

Near-death studies in the past have focused on adults. The classical model that emerged was an adult model—of adults, for adults. What is lacking has been an *in-depth* study of near-death states as seen *through the eyes of the child experiencer* beyond the initial work done by Melvin Morse, M.D., and chronicled in his book *Closer to the Light: Learning from the Near-Death Experiences of Children.*[3] Because of this, the fuller story of what happens to kids has been bypassed. In seeking to remedy the situation, I made a most amazing discovery: child experiencers of near-death states have all the markers to indicate that they are the precursors, the advance wave, who not only set the stage for the millennial generation but also offer persuasive evidence to indicate that a new race is aborning—evolution in our lifetime.

A poll taken by *U.S. News & World Report* in early 1997 estimates that there are fifteen million near-death experiencers in the United States,[4] or about one-third of those who "died" but later revived. That already high figure does *not* take into account child experiencers. The best estimate we have for kids comes from the work of Morse. He reported the occurrence rate for youngsters at around 70 percent, more than double that of the adult population.

In other words, *the vast majority of children who face death experience a near-death scenario. And these children contend with the same aftereffects, both psychological and physiological, as do adults . . . but in a different manner. Good and evil jumble together for them, and the line separating one reality from another disappears.*

Modern technology and ever-improving resuscitation techniques are returning more people from the brink of death, especially children, than even ten years ago. We've already explored adult versions of encountering the Other Side; now it's time to focus on kids. Except that, when we talk about little ones, we must also address evolutionary factors. Actually, any reference to near-death states, whether concerning adults or kids, can no longer be limited to an analysis of "the experience" as a single, anomalous event—because it isn't.

Near-death states comprise a complex and many-faceted phenomenon that is part of a much larger genre, *transformations of consciousness*. As such, they model broader issues that impinge upon the human family as a whole. Label them evolution's nod, God's will, or the adaptation of the species; whatever they're called, the experience and its aftereffects are reflective of a powerful force for change that is undeniable in its impact.

Recent attacks on Charles Darwin's theory of evolution put what I have just said into perspective. Bear with me as I show you why.

Darwin based his theory on the doctrine of uniformitarianism, which states that all geological phenomena may be explained as the result of existing forces operating uniformly from the origin of life on earth to the present, and that biological advancement from species to species is equally gradual and caused by similar forces.

How then, ask Michael Cremo and Richard Thompson, authors of *Forbidden Archaeology: The Hidden History of the Human Race*,[5] do you explain the existence of an ornate vase inlaid with silver embedded in rock over five hundred million years old? And how, asks Richard Milton, author of *Shattering the Myths of Darwinism*,[6] can you account for the many examples of rapidly forming fossils (e.g., that of a fish formed as it was swallowed by another fish, or of an ancient amphibian in the process of giving birth), and rocks off Britain's coast that took shape in a matter of hours rather than millions of years?

Thanks to computer modeling, satellite photography, and a new breed of scientist willing to ask the unthinkable, a new theory of evolution is developing—one based on evidence from the fossil record in rock strata—that posits that the earth has suffered severe convulsions, volcanic upheavals, and worldwide flooding at various stages in its prehistory. These catastrophes, and the *sudden changes* that resulted, are proving to have been a greater influence on the path evolution took than graduated pressure over time.

The brilliant paleontologist Stephen Jay Gould applied the catastrophe theory to species adaptation by detailing how a species can go for millions of years without change and then, within a brief span, perhaps a hundred years or much less, make a *quantum leap* in evolution and accomplish the impossible.

Sudden changes. Quantum leaps. *Evolution can alter its direction in a heartbeat*—transforming geological formations, continents, plants, animals, human beings, even us moderns—irrespective of the natural order.

None of the present theories on evolution addresses biochemical molecules. Found at the core of the tiniest lifeforms, biochemical molecules, the "living machinery of consciousness," *know and are uniquely sensitive to light*. According to Michael J. Behe, associate professor of biochemistry at Lehigh University in Pennsylvania and author of *Darwin's Black Box: The Biochemical Challenge to Evolution,*[7] "Light sensitivity could not have evolved, but must have been designed by some form of prior intelligence."

Intelligent design, responsible for the encoding of light sensitivity and a knowingness of light in all life-forms, accommodates evolution's nod as if responding to a greater plan, one that is replete with growth contingencies.

Take entropy, for instance. Contrary to its definition as the law of diminishing order and the decreased availability of energy, entropy *always* leads to new forms and a higher order—as illustrated by chaos mathematics. This theory tells us that in any system where unpredictability suddenly increases to the point that order disintegrates into chaos, that very chaos gives birth to new order. *Life utilizes random unpredictability to guarantee continuous change and advancement.*

Evolution operates the same way in the human family.

Always, sudden changes, quantum leaps in physiology and consciousness, have catapulted the growth and development of humankind beyond that which can be explained. As "missing links" are still standard fare in trying to understand the evolution of our bodies, so, too, are there missing connectors in any attempt to rationalize the evolution of consciousness.

Until now.

My work in the sixties and early seventies researching altered and transformed states of consciousness, and since 1978 studying near-death states, has enabled me to recognize that these experiences have less to do with anything paranormal, religious, mystical, or offering proof of an afterlife than they do with how evolution might really work.

I have come to realize that what is involved in a transformation of consciousness, whether precipitated by the cataclysm of a near-death experience or a shamanic vision quest or a kundalini breakthrough or a baptism of the Holy Spirit, is a structural, chemical, and functional change that occurs in the brain. This sudden change, sometimes akin to a quantum leap, flings the experiencer from one mode of existence to another—as if on cue. Social justice and moral integrity take on the vigor of "new light" when this occurs.

I call the phenomenon a *brain shift/spirit shift,* and I suspect that, because of the gravity of its aftereffects, such a shift is the engine that drives evolution—that which transforms, transmutes, and advances our species while triggering the development of the higher brain.

This suspicion of mine is based on the interviews *and* observations I have conducted with over 3,000 adult near-death experiencers (not counting the significant others I also spoke with), as well as nearly the same number of people who had undergone transformations of consciousness through other means; this research base was expanded by work with 277 child experiencers (about half still youngsters, the rest having reached their teen or adult years).

Since near-death states model consciousness transformations in a neutral fashion, as they happen to anyone, at any age, under any condition, anywhere, I will use my research in this field to explore the broader subject of brain shift/spirit shift and what that implies.

Before I do, it would be helpful if I commented on why and how I do research. I was "told" during my third near-death experience that it would be my job, when I returned to life, to bring clarity and perspective to what I had just survived while testing the validity of its revelation. Thus, it has never been my intent or interest to verify or challenge anyone else's findings. As fate would have it, however, my research has indeed become a challenge to the generally accepted classical model.

The protocol I use is that of a police investigator, a skill I learned from my police-officer father (that's why some people call me the gumshoe of near-death). I specialize in interviews *and* observations, cross-checking everything I notice a minimum of four times with different people in different sections of the country, as a way to ensure that any bias I may have as a near-death experiencer will not cloud my perception and that my work is not completely dependent on anecdote. Questionnaires for me are auxiliary, used only to further examine certain aspects of near-death states. All of my work is original, and most of it has since been verified by other researchers. Near-death studies has been a full-time profession for me since 1978, in addition to employment that pays for the groceries.

My interview style is straightforward. I ask open-ended questions, such as "What happened to you?" If I want to know more, I signal that intent with forward body movement, a tilt of my head, a smile, and the incredibly magical word "and . . ." Language used is determined by the experiencer as he or she responds to questions. To obtain a greater depth of material, I learned early on to avoid telling anyone I was a researcher, and to rely more on facial expressions and body posturing than on words. I watch as well as listen, ever mindful of feelings and sensations, for the dance we humans engage in as we relate to one another is quite revealing.

I altered my style somewhat with children, in this manner: no parents were allowed when I was with them; the same eye-level contact was maintained throughout the interviews; I replaced note-taking with gentleness; I encouraged them to share *feelings* as well as memories; and I opened myself to sense the wave of consciousness they rode.

Parents were interviewed too, as I wanted to know their point of view and whether they might have applied any pressure on their child by making a big deal out of it. This is important, as children are capable of slanting their stories to fit the emotional expectations of their parents and/or teachers. If I suspected such a compromise had been made, I would retire the account to the dustbin. I rejected about 15 percent of the interview opportunities I had with children for this reason. Fascination with "out of the mouths of babes" reports can mislead more readily than enlighten.

But these claims can also be right on target, as a report from Richmond, Virginia, demonstrates. In February 1996, a mother with two small daughters aboard lost control of her car and flipped it over into a ditch. The oldest nearly lost a leg, and three-year-old Victoria died. Refusing the grim verdict, a police officer began CPR (cardiopulmonary resuscitation) on the lifeless body. Five minutes later the little girl breathed. Her first words were: "I saw Jesus. But he told me it wasn't my time and I need to go back and be with my daddy." The child's grandfather, a man who drank heavily and "messed around," was so overcome by Victoria's message that he quit drinking and started to read the Bible. (This report is from Pat Kennedy, a friend of Victoria's family.)

Why are we so awestruck with what children have to say? Because we've forgotten what it is like to be one.

In 1994, I devised a lengthy questionnaire to probe the memories of those who had had a near-death episode as a child. My goal was not only to test recall, but to track the aftereffects throughout various life stages. Of the fifty-two people who participated, forty-four had experienced the near-death phenomenon by their fifteenth birthday. The youngest to fill out the questionnaire was twelve, the oldest a seventy-two-year-old who had been pronounced clinically dead at four and a half.

Because questionnaire findings so closely mirror what I have observed throughout the bulk of my work, I will reference them often and provide direct quotes. Each time a quote appears, the experiencer's name (a few requested anonymity), location, age of occurrence, and cause will be noted. For starters:

Francis Piekarski, New Martinsville, West Virginia. NDE at age five from drowning; at twelve from high fever and bone infection. "I got a bone infection and my temperature shot up to 105 degrees. I was very sick and my body began to shake. My mother was scared. So as not to scare her more, I stiffened up my muscles to stop the shaking. All of a sudden my body shook violently. My mother ran from the room yelling, 'He's dying.' At that moment, I was out of my body and looking up from the foot of my bed. I saw two men in their mid-twenties. One was looking to the left and the other to the right. They were about ten feet tall. It made me feel better that they were there. I felt they were angels and were guarding me."

Carl Allen Pierson, Hinton, West Virginia. NDE at age eight or nine, hit by lightning. "During a thunderstorm, with a metal washtub over my head, I went to untie a cow from the tree for my uncle. When I got approximately fifteen feet from the tree, lightning hit it and bounced to the tub. I was barefoot, standing on wet grass. Lightning took all the galvanizing off the tub, and knocked me and the tub away from the tree. The tub traveled about 250 feet and it knocked me 25 feet away. Burned me everywhere that I had contact with the tub. Turned the tub black. I was hovering above as my family encircled my body, which was lying on the grass. It was communicated that I was dead. I was trying to tell them I was not dead, but I made no sounds. Soft light. Warm glowing feeling. Something or someone told me that everything would be okay, then there was blackness. Next I was lying in a dark house on a couch but could not hear or see, yet I was aware of what was going on. I could not move anything, like my body muscles were locked up. Great pain. Blackness. Then I was in a hospital or doctor's office on a gurney. I had a vision and saw myself hovering over my body again, but this time no one was present. My body was larger (adult size). I remember hearing the news on the radio, something about a boy who had been killed by lightning.

There was mention of it in the local paper, too. Both turned out to be false reports, as you can readily see."

Barbara True Bradley, Des Moines, Iowa. NDE at age four and a half, pneumonia, complications from surgery. "I was in the hospital with lobar pneumonia and a pus pocket in the lung, along with an extremely high fever. In 1926 there was no sulfa or penicillin. The doctors told my mother I was critically ill. I had two operations. Two of my ribs were removed in order to open my lung and keep it open for the pus to be siphoned out several times a day. It was painful and frightening for a little kid! Sometime during this illness, my mother was told that that particular night would be the turning point. She and the Episcopal pastor prayed over me all night. I was better the next day. My 'dream' happened that night, although I'm not sure. This 'dream' was in black and white frames except one picture of me all dressed up in skirt, sweater, hose, and heels, and wearing a yellow carnation, going to a football game. (At the time my family lived in Nebraska—Big Red Country. Later, when I married, my husband and I moved to Iowa—Yellow and Black Country.) In other scenes I saw myself walking toward the rear of an airplane that had two seats on each side of one aisle. I rode on a train that had a glass-domed top with pine and birch trees flashing by outside. (According to my encyclopedia, the first glass-domed train ran in 1945.) I watched myself being married to a dark-haired man in front of an altar that had a cross in the back. I had long, dark hair and wore a white dress with a white veil and a long train. Everything subsequently happened as shown to me."

John Raymond Liona, Brooklyn, New York. Complications at birth. "I was strangled by my umbilical cord during birth.

Once born, I was given a tracheotomy to get me breathing—black eyes, swollen face, cuts from forceps. My mother didn't see me until the third day. I relive the event in my dreams from time to time, vividly. I remember being bent over or kneeling down, fighting with these knots. I was very upset and angry. Just when I was thinking I was getting in control of these things, I got hit in the face (the doc with the forceps). I started struggling even more. All of a sudden I became very peaceful. Everything I was feeling before just poured out of me and I was so calm. I remember looking at my hands, but the details are not clear. I think I was floating, because I was trying to move forward but could not. I was trying to reach this woman in the distance. The material of her gown was glowing with little specks of light trailing off. There was a buzzing or humming sound. She floated away toward the left. I was calling to her, yelling, but the light, it was all around. It was coming from the right, and was so bright. She could not hear me. I was so upset, as I wanted to go with her."

Tonecia Maxine McMillan, Oxon Hill, Maryland. NDE at age eleven, drowning. "I was on an inner tube in the water off a beach in Delaware. I had ventured out too far. My grandmother (who raised me, as I never lived with my siblings) motioned for me to come back to shore. I misjudged the depth. I stepped out of the inner tube and began to drown. I left my body. I could see myself in the water. I saw my grandmother trying to come and get me, and I saw my brother cut his left foot. Then I was in a very beautiful, peaceful, picturesque place like a meadow. I felt very loved. The colors were brilliant; they were nothing like I have ever seen before. There is simply no comparison—the yellows, greens—so very beautiful, so peaceful. At the time of my drowning, I was on a 'black beach,' so to speak. Delaware still was practicing segregation. I was told that two white men were on the beach at the time. These two men saved my life by pulling me to shore, then *they simply disappeared.* On the way to the hospital, when I asked my brother how his cut foot was doing, I was met with stony silence. He couldn't deal with the fact that I saw his accident while I was out of my body."

Anell Q. Tubbs, Boise, Idaho. NDE at age seven or eight, blow to head. "I was playing on a hassock in the living room. It rolled and I fell off backward, striking the base of my head on the sharp corner of the coffee table—right in the little area where the neck and skull attach. Everything went black and there was this *whoosh,* and I felt like I was traveling at an extremely high rate of speed through the blackness. Then, in a split second, I relived my entire life, every bit of it, and it was in color just like it was happening all over again— emotions and all—but it only took a split second. The next thing I remember is sitting up and thinking, 'So that is what

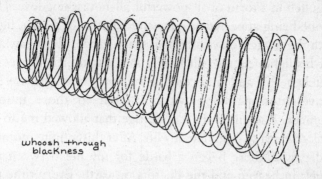

whoosh through
blackness

it is like to die.' I don't remember telling anyone. But it has always been fresh and right in the front of my mind."

Laura, San Francisco, California. NDE at age three and a half, child abuse, surgery. "My father, in a blind drunken rage, raped and sodomized and beat me to death in the middle of the night. At the most extreme outpost of pain, I cried out to God and in that moment I was torn from life. As I died I felt myself raised up by angels in robes of many colors. I did not know where they were taking me as they flew, carrying me up higher and higher in the sky. Finally, we reached a place where emptiness gave way to form, and form took the shape of huge cloudlike masses on which other angels seemed to be walking, although they too floated through the air. The angels carrying me lay me at the feet of a beautiful female angel whose radiating love was more powerful than any of those around her. She said to me in a voice whose sweetness and tone are unknown here on earth, 'Tell me your story.' I said to her, not in spoken words but in thoughts, 'I will, but now I need to rest.' My spirit had no energy, even to answer this loving lady. God in the manifestation of infinite light appeared off to my left, and I was engulfed in a form of all-powerful, all-nourishing love. That divine being appeared as a massive column of golden light, with the suggestion of a human shape inside. I both saw and felt his light, feeling as if I were in a warm bath that completely healed and protected me. I never wanted to leave. No conversation passed between us, but in those infinite moments I acquired the knowledge that allowed me to go back to earth to complete my life. After this infinite moment had passed, there began a battle for my life between the angels in heaven and the doctors on earth. Every time the doctors pounded on my chest, my spirit was sucked into my body for a split second, only to be pulled back again by the angels. They held me by my feet, struggling to keep me from coming back. Finally, the doctors pounded one last time. I heard an angel say, 'They're stronger than we are,' and I was sucked back into my body, sat up, screamed, and passed out. To this day, I always have the feeling that I need to go back, that there was something more I was meant to do there before returning. That feeling of incompleteness keeps me half in the other world all the time."

Regina Patrick, Toledo, Ohio. NDE at age four, pneumonia. "From infancy until I was ten years old, I was chronically in and out of the hospital. At age four, it was because of pneumonia. It was night and I lay on my stomach, having just awakened from what I took for a dream. A group of five to ten ethereal people had just given me a lot of instructions. The instructions were important and I needed to remember them. I was trying, but there were so many that I couldn't. I even tried repeating them to myself again and again, but to no avail. I was getting them jumbled and confused. I sensed that these instructions would be important to me someday, even if I didn't understand them. I was starting to get frustrated. Just at that moment, we separated. Because there was no sense of movement, I can't say whether I moved away from them or they from me, or if we separated from each other simultaneously. I awoke with a strange thing, something I had never had before, a great sense of peace, which confused me. What was the purpose of this peace? Normally, when I awoke in the hospital like this, I worried about my family back home: What were they doing? Were they worried about me? Were they okay? The peace obliterated my worry. I tried again to remember what they had told me but found I could remember even less now that I was awake. I was concerned that 'they' (the ethereal people) would be mad at me for forgetting their message."

TWO

BRAIN SHIFT/ SPIRIT SHIFT

There is a soul force in the universe, which if we permit it will flow through us and produce miraculous results.

Mahatma Gandhi

The "engine" of evolution, that force that drives the adaptation and refinement of species, is normally so gradual that centuries must pass before we can even glimpse the changes it fosters. Brain shifts/spirit shifts jump-start that process in the human family. They are in essence evolution's quantum leap, in the way experiencers are affected by the resulting cascades of aftereffects.

These two shifts are the invisible weights that tip perceptual scales toward spiritual realities instead of physical actualities. Whereas brain shifts can be examined, verified, and explained, at least to some degree, spirit shifts can be identified only by interpreting responses; that is, by recognizing the type of behavioral changes exhibited by the experiencer.

Among adult experiencers, I regard a brain shift/spirit shift as a growth event—a sudden, unexpected twist in life that operates like a "washing machine" in how it motivates us to clean up our habits, flush out our minds, and overhaul our lifestyles. Some examples of growth events are: losing when we were certain we would win, or winning when we were certain we would lose; being forced to slow down in life when we wanted to go faster, or being speeded up when we wanted to go slow; suffering when we wanted to prosper, or prospering when we were unprepared or even unwilling. Growth events, if we are open to the messages they would impart, not only give us the opportunity to turn our lives around but allow us to make course corrections in favor of that which is spiritual. Growth events engendered by the near-death phenomenon are unusually powerful and far-reaching in their impact.

Among child experiencers, I regard a brain shift/spirit shift as an evolutionary event—for, regardless of how others are affected by a child's near-death scenario, the second birth the child seems to undergo reorders or "seeds" the youngster in ways that are exceptional to regular behavior development. Also, the brain is affected to a greater degree in children than in adults, propelling them into abstractions and learning enhancements as creative expression soars. This marks them as different from their agemates and at variance with family and social structures. Once grown, they attempt to enter the traditional workforce with a nontraditional mindset, ever pushing for change and new, even exotic, options and alternatives. The "second-born" challenge every aspect of society on every level, continuously. They inspire the kind of cultural growth that fuels social revolution.

To advance the idea that at the core of near-death episodes and other similar states is a brain shift/spirit shift, we need to explore the subject from various angles (as does the report *Phase II—Brain Shift/Spirit Shift: A Theoretical Model Using Research on Near-Death States to Explore the Transformation of Consciousness*).[1]

BRAIN SHIFT

Any manner of occurrence can trigger a brain shift. I would include here those of a more turbulent nature, such as: religious conversions, near-death episodes, kundalini breakthroughs, shamanistic vision quests, sudden spiritual transformations, certain types of head trauma, or having been hit by lightning. I would also count those more tranquil in how they are experienced—like the slow, steady application of spiritual disciplines, mindfulness techniques, meditation, sacred rituals, or a prayerful state of mind in which an individual simply desires to become a better person.

With turbulent experiences, I have noticed that the brain organ (structure, chemistry, function) seems to shift before the mind, or the degree of consciousness present. With tranquil experiences, the mind, or consciousness level, tends to shift before the brain.

Which shifts first makes a difference with the aftereffects: tranquil episodes are gradual and usually happen in increments, giving a person time mentally to think and prepare; turbulent ones are so immediate and so powerful that the brain organ itself can be overwhelmed, compounding the challenges of whatever might be encountered. Certain major characteristics tend to be displayed by people who have gone through a brain shift.

Physiological Aftereffects
Changes in thought processing (switch from sequential/ selective thinking to clustered thinking and an acceptance of ambiguity)
Insatiable curiosity
Heightened intelligence

More creativity and inventiveness

Unusual sensitivity to light and sound

Substantially more or less energy (even energy surges, often more sexual)

Reversal of body clock

Lower blood pressure

Accelerated metabolic and substance absorption rates (decreased tolerance of pharmaceuticals and chemically treated products)

Electrical sensitivity

Synesthesia (multiple sensing)

Increased allergies or sensitivities

A preference for more vegetables and grains (less meat)

Physically younger appearance (before and after photos can differ)

Psychological Aftereffects

Loss of the fear of death

More spiritual/less religious

Able to abstract easily

Philosophical

Possible bouts of depression

Disregard for time

More generous and charitable

Capable of forming expansive concepts of love while at the same time challenged in initiating and maintaining satisfying relationships

Exaggerated "inner child" issues

Less competitive

Convinced of a life purpose

Rejection of previous limitations and norms

Heightened sensations of taste, touch, texture, and smell

Increased psychic ability and future memory episodes

Charismatic
Childlike sense of wonder and joy
Less stressed
More detached and objective (dissociation)
"Merge" easily (absorption)
Hunger for knowledge and learning

Note that these characteristics can be positive or negative, depending on how they are applied. Based on my previous investigations of spiritual awakenings and enlightenment done in the 1960s and 1970s, these characteristics match across the board with the universal experience of a transforming and evolving consciousness—in other words, a brain shift.

This listing highlights the aftereffects that are normal and typical to a brain shift. Because of the intensity of impact, it takes about seven years for the average adult experiencer to fully integrate them. With kids, it depends—some adjust quickly, others not until they reach adulthood.

Almost every single one of the aftereffects can be traced to enhanced, accelerated limbic system involvement as a point of origination in the brain. For this reason, it would behoove us to learn something about this little-known area.

THE LIMBIC SYSTEM AND EMOTIONS

The limbic system, a conglomerate of various small but important brain structures located in a semicircle in the middle of the brain, caps off the topmost extension of the brain stem. It wraps around our primitive reptilian brain, translating our basic instincts for sex, hunger, sleep, fear, and survival into more flexible and social forms of behavior. Often referred to as the emotional or feeling center (the "gut brain"), the limbic system is also the seat of the immune system and the body's ability to heal itself. Few people realize that it is the limbic system that operates as the "executive office" in deciding what information is stored in memory, what is forgotten, and what will be further elaborated upon and refined in the two main hemispheres and throughout the brain/mind assembly. And it has a direct neural connection to the heart.

Although this small but extremely efficient system has been part of us for hundreds of thousands of years of brain evolution, only recently has it been recognized as the most complicated structure on earth. Many brain researchers now believe that if the limbic system doesn't actually originate "mind," then it certainly is the gateway within the brain to higher realms of mind and more powerfully diverse and collective types of consciousness. Thus, the staging arena where the organ called the brain accesses and filters what is referred to as the mind *is the limbic system*.

The brain, incidentally, has been discovered to be more emotional than cognitive. Nicholas Humphrey, a senior research fellow at Cambridge University, has explained, "A person can be conscious without thinking anything. But a person simply cannot be conscious without feeling."[2] Combine this with the scientific finding that feedback between the limbic system and the heart is *instantaneous,* and it becomes clear why in most near-death scenarios experiencers are "flooded with love."

THE LIMBIC SYSTEM AND CHANGES IN THE BRAIN

When the limbic is stimulated, it leaves "prints." With a little bit of stimulation, we get excited, perk up, emotions flow, and receptivity is enhanced (music, rituals, and celebrations promote such a response). Passion/compassion turns on with more stimulation, along with displays of psychic/

intuitive abilities and the inspiration to take action (hearing charismatic speakers and reading shocking news headlines often accomplish this; for instance, listening to the speeches of Martin Luther King, Jr., or hearing of the tragic death of Princess Diana). Massive surges of love and light, faculty extensions, panoramic visions, and the emergence of wisdom and knowing can occur when the limbic system is deeply impacted by a sudden change or intense shift.

When the limbic system is "spun around" or receives a good "blow," it's as if the temporal lobes, nervous system, and heart are signaled to do one of two things: shut down or accelerate function. Shutting down means damage or death. Accelerated function means healing or enhancement. What we refer to as "the aftereffects" in cases of near-death and near-death-like states may well be the *cascade effect,* or "imprinting," that various bodily systems come to exhibit in reaction to and in correspondence with the specifics of limbic enhancement/enlargement/acceleration. The extent of the cascade effect seems to reveal the degree to which the limbic system was impacted.

The limbic system, far from being just a survival center, jump-starts:

LEARNING "When emotions do not guide our awareness of the environment, thoughts, dreams, and images disappear. Our most subtle feelings have a physical basis within the limbic region, and the limbic should never be forgotten."[3]

EMOTING "The intensity of electrical current surrounding the heart's activity is about fifty times more powerful than that of the brain organ and precedes hemispheric action. There is 'heart intelligence' in how the heart gives intuitive input to the mind."[4]

And the limbic system, once accelerated in function, is the gateway of initiation for such conditions as:

MULTIPLE SENSING (SYNESTHESIA) Multisensory awareness, like hearing paintings, smelling sounds, tasting vision, seeing music. Neurologist Richard E. Cytowic believes sensing in multiple ways is not something new but has always existed and can be developed by anyone.[5]

CLUSTERED THINKING "Shaking together" or "clustering" information, instead of using linear logic, so data can be rearranged and tossed around in new ways; a sign of genius. Psychologist Howard Gardner speaks of Einstein seeing a light ray in his mind and knowing he was right, French composer Olivier Messiaen seeing color in tones, and Picasso experiencing numbers as patterns of contour.[6]

PARALLEL PROCESSING/SIMULTANEOUS BRAIN WAVES Presence of all brain-wave speeds (beta, alpha, theta, and delta) in simultaneous operation; the "awakened" mind. Anna Wise, a researcher of brain waves, and Max Cade, a psychobiologist and biophysicist, found that spiritual adepts can utilize the full range of brain-wave levels simultaneously. Wise discovered that certain images, words, and timed pauses could actually shift anyone's brain into this state.[7]

MIND OVER MATTER Moving physical objects with brain-wave emissions. Scientists at the New York State Department of Health, Albany, have discovered that people using thought alone can move a computer cursor around a display screen. Clinical trials are in progress to see if paralyzed individuals can be taught the same technique to help them communicate better and perform simple tasks.[8]

Any experience that overwhelms a person to the degree that thought processes are altered appreciably changes brain structure to some extent. We know this from clinical experiments using PET scans (positron-emission tomography). Near-death states and other transformative episodes of the same or similar magnitude affect an individual even more, engendering in most cases evidence to suggest permanent bodymind changes—accompanied by the awakening of higher levels of consciousness.

"Growth spurts" in the brain (intelligence and/or faculty enhancements) appear to be the result of brain cell branches *suddenly* increasing in number and spreading rapidly, which expands contact between cells. Scientists have long suspected that any rise in intelligence has more to do with these spurts than with the brain hemispheres (left and right) and neocortex (new or high brain). *Growth spurts* (or heightened brain cell branching) *literally rewire and reconfigure the brain,* making more complex, efficient neural pathways for transmitting information. Everything else proceeds from this factor—the brain and how it shifts structure and chemistry to suit the demands of new modes of usage.

THE TEMPORAL LOBES AND THINGS "FUTURE"

While studying cases of child experiencers, I came across clusters of reports at certain ages. Determining how significant these age clusters are requires larger studies than mine, but, for the present, my statistics suffice to support an intriguing observation: there appears to be a connection between the ages when most near-death episodes occur in kids and the more critical stages of childhood brain development.

Age Clusters Found in Reported Cases of a Brain Shift

Age Clusters	Correlations
CHILDREN AND YOUNG ADULTS	
*Birth– 15 months	When the actual wiring of the brain is determined and synapse formation increases 20-fold; utilizes more than twice the energy of an adult brain.
*3–5 years	Time of temporal lobe development; explore and experiment with possible roles, future patterns, action/reaction, environmental continuity.
7–9 years	Time of judgment/discrimination development; often when serious accidents and illnesses occur, or problems with significant others.
11–15 years	Time of puberty; hormone fluctuations; sexuality and authority questioned; identity crisis.
MATURE ADULTS	
†27–32 years	Crossover between adherence to values of friends, family, and the pressures of the workplace and the urge to establish self as an independent and mature ego; social crisis.

Note: Among mature adults, smaller clusters are notable around the ages of 39, 49, and 59. Children's data are based on 1997 analysis; adults, on 1994 analysis. More research is needed for reliable confirmation of these groupings.

* With children, the first two age categories are where most of the reports cluster in my research base, as well as where I found the most compelling cases of genius.
† With adults, I found the largest cluster from ages 27 to 32.

Although it comes from my work with near-death survivors, I use the term "brain shift" in the chart to reflect a broader range of inquiry, because large numbers of unusual incidents involving children cluster at the same ages as do the near-death reports in my research, especially with youngsters aged three to five.

I first began tracking anomalous events in the mid-sixties out of pure curiosity and noticed, much to my surprise, that three- to five-year-olds were much more apt than persons of any other age to experience past-life recall, alien sightings, alien abductions, flying dreams, out-of-body episodes, spirit visitations, invisible friends, and other paranormal and psychic occurrences. This is the *same time frame* when long-term memory begins for most children and when storytelling has the greatest influence. It is also the period when kids are almost entirely *future oriented* and temporal lobe development predominates. (The temporal lobes are those sections of the brain located at or near the temples.) Traditionally, the temporal lobes are referred to as the "patterning center," that place where our original blueprints of shape and form are stored. For this reason, they are thought to be the seat of imagination.

Because youngsters who have near-death experiences come to have an extraordinary relationship with things future, I searched through studies done on childhood behavior development for anything that might explain why—and learned that kids between three and five have no natural sense of time or space. They gain this sense *by projecting into the future* and by intuitively engaging with futuristic ideas, images, feelings, and sensations. The future does not appear as "future" to children. To them it is simply another aspect of "now" (that which is immediate), and it remains so until they are able to establish the validity of continuous scenery and connected wholes. Once they accomplish this, they have the perspective and the sense of continuity they need to adapt to ever-changing environments and the meaningfulness of cause and effect (consequences). In other words, the imaginal adventures of childhood are *necessary* for the development of healthy minds.

Yet near-death states that happen during this same juncture in brain development appear to accelerate mental growth in child experiencers years ahead of what would be expected. Perhaps this critical timing is the reason. More than just imaginal worlds and magical imagery are involved in near-death states, though. The shift child experiencers undergo suggests the hand of evolution at work.

A fascinating fact is that adults as well as children who have undergone any type of brain shift regularly begin to "step" into the future. Many even begin to "live" the future ahead of time and remember their experience when the futuristic event actually occurs. Their feat mimics what happens to ordinary kids between the ages of three and five. I called this the "future memory" phenomenon and wrote a book about it,[9] defining the phenomenon as:

Future Memory: to live in advance (subjective/sensory rich). The ability to fully live a given event or sequence of events in subjective reality before living the same episode in objective reality. This is usually, but not always, forgotten by the individual after it occurs, only to be remembered later when some "signal" triggers memory. Sensory-rich future memory is so detailed as to include movements, thoughts, smells, tastes, decisions, sights, and sounds of regular physical living. All this is actually lived and physically, emotionally, and sensorially experienced, *not* merely watched (which is clairvoyance), heard (clairaudience), predicted (prophecy), or known (precognition); and that living is so thorough, there is no way to distinguish it from everyday reality while the phenomenon is in progress.

Future memory is not to be confused with déjà vu, which is past oriented. What I refer to is a clear and cogent ability to somehow access the future and "live" it *before* physical manifestation. That sense of "living in advance" is acutely felt by experiencers. Some examples from interviews with adults:

A former military officer who now lives in Illinois pre-experiences conversations at meetings he attends. He claims this relaxes him and makes life more interesting.

A woman in Washington State is able to comfort troubled travelers because she prelives which bus and plane terminals to visit and who to look for and why.

A woman in Alabama meets fellow shoppers in advance and preexperiences standing at cash registers, and seeing items rung up at other registers, including prices.

Distinguishing features of the future memory phenomenon are: *physical sensation at start and finish,* akin to a chill, rush, lift, tickle, or "high" (a signal of brain-chemical release); *pattern of occurrence,* universal regardless of experiencer; *mind state when it happens,* usually wide awake and alert, although some report having it during dream states; *content,* almost always mundane activity, but can cover significant events—feels as if it's a rehearsal of some kind; *awareness of power to change the future divided afterward,* with some claiming the pre-lived future can be changed, others saying it can't; *consequences,* handling stress better because of rehearsals, becoming more peaceful and confident—frequency of episodes tends to subside once experiencer feels more grounded.

The similarities between what happens naturally to children from ages three to five and what happens to experiencers of any age after a brain shift, once they begin having future memory episodes, is uncanny. Consider these striking comparisons.

Childhood Brain Development and the Brain Shift Experience

Typical Three- to Five-Year-Olds	*Adult and Child Brain Shift Experiencers*
Temporal Lobe Development Emerging Consciousness	*Temporal Lobe Expansion* Enlarging Consciousness
Prelive the future on a regular basis, spend more time in future than in present.	Prelive the future on a regular basis through dream states, visions, future memory episodes.
Play with futuristic possibilities as a way of "getting ready"; rehearse in advance demands soon to be made upon them.	Preexperience life's challenges and opportunities before they occur as a way of preparing for demands they will soon face.
No natural understanding of time-space states; consider "future" an aspect of "now." Gain perspective and continuity by establishing the validity of action/ reaction or "future" (continuous scenery and connected wholes).	No longer restricted by a sense of time-space states; an aware-ness of simultaneity and the importance of "now." Embrace broader dimensions of experi-ence beyond that of "future" (unlimited perspectives held in tandem with the continuity of stable reference points).
Progress from mental imagery of universal archetypes to cultural stereotypes in a process of self-discovery.	Progress from mental imagery of cultural stereotypes to the individuation process in a journey of soul discovery.
The Birth of Imagination	*The Rebirth of Imagination*

This chart emphasizes how reliable the future memory phenomenon may be as a signal that a person's brain is in the process of shifting in structure, chemistry, and function; that it's undergoing a growth spurt. And that, as part of the shift, experiencers tend to *revert back to the brain-development stage of three- to five-year-olds,* and I believe for the same reason: *to reestablish continuity and order through futuristic rehearsals* so they can ready themselves for the greater challenge of higher mind states and spiritual maturity. I have observed that:

> Being able to live the future in advance, and remember that one did, alleviates much of the stress and fear that worrying about unknown variables can cause. This advanced preparation enables the human psyche to negotiate the demands of sudden change more smoothly. The ability imparts an immense sense of confidence and peace in individuals, no matter what age, and often leads to frequent incidences of synchronicity (meaningful "coincidences") as if one's life were caught up in some type of "flow."[10]

THE TEMPORAL LOBES AND IMAGERY

Todd Murphy, himself a near-death survivor, researches near-death imagery cross-culturally. In his paper "The Structure and Function of Near-Death Experiences: An Algorithmic Hypothesis,"[11] he states:

> It is well established that, although there appears to be a universal *grammar* to NDEs, the specific *vocabulary* of any given case is determined by a variety of factors including age, culture, the specific circumstances in which the patient dies, psychological history, and possibly many other, still undiscovered factors. A dictionary containing this vocabulary might encompass the whole of human subjectivity including our symbolism, myths, and religions.

In discussions with Murphy, he reminded me that the left temporal lobe specializes in negative emotions and images (things fear based, like paranoia and sorrow), while the expertise of the right temporal lobe is with positive emotions and images (things love based, as joy and peace). Two excellent sources of scientific material on this subject are the article "Toward a Psychobiology of Transcendence: God in the Brain," by Arnold J. Mandell,[12] and the book *Neuropsychological Bases of God Beliefs,* by Michael A. Persinger.[13]

Persinger induced pleasant, heavenlike near-death experiences in subjects by stimulating the Sylvian fissure in the right temporal lobe. He used magnetic signals of the same strength as those produced by the earth's magnetic field to accomplish the feat. Because his work had results similar to that of Wilder Penfield, a medical doctor probing certain parts of the brain during surgery to target memory recall,[14] many researchers are now convinced that unpleasant/hellish near-death states are a product of exciting the left temporal lobe and pleasant/heavenly ones, the right.

Persinger's experiments and those of physicians like Penfield, however, *failed* to induce anything other than a *generalized pattern* of imagery, a basic template or "blueprint." This was also true with similar states caused by temporal lobe seizure, centrifuge pilot training, and excessive stress. The fact that classical near-death scenarios are easily created was undoubtedly a major impetus behind Raymond Moody's study of crystal or mirror gazing. Through resurrecting the centuries-old practice, he had hoped to see if volunteers really could contact the Other Side and experience a legitimate "visitation." His book *Reunions: Visionary Encounters with Departed Loved Ones*[15] caused quite a stir, to say the least, and did result in a few claims of success.

Even so, *no researcher or experiencer of any such created imagery/episode,* including Moody, *has ever induced or exhibited the full scope and impact of genuine near-death states, the incredible range of detail present in most of them* (which only on rare occasions could have been known about in advance), *nor the spread of aftereffects* (which in most cases increase with time and become permanent).

All anyone can accomplish when stimulating the temporal lobes (left or right), regardless of method or conditions, is to create *general pattern arrangements* of emotions and images. The reason for this is straightforward enough: the temporal lobes are storage receptacles of basic shapes, forms, feelings, and sounds. Implicit in this is the notion that together they may function as a resource center or data comparison device that children can tap into as they learn to discern differences. As we age, engaging in creative imagination and invention ensures that both lobes not only remain active but can take on more expansive and expressive projects.

But if mind states alter significantly, as during a brain shift, the temporal lobes seem to assume the role of *mediator between worlds.* This "mediator within" is strongly evident in near-death cases. Initial imagery, sometimes called "overleafs," will *always* match what will accommodate the experiencer's most urgent need at the moment, and/or what will directly affect those around him or her. This phenomenon of accommodation occurs repeatedly, regardless of whether the imagery features God or religious figures or angels, animals, relatives, or friends.

This leads me to believe that the initial patterning of any otherworld journey is first and foremost to either relax the experiencer and put him or her at ease (through a pleasant episode), or tense the experiencer and alert him or her (through an unpleasant episode), so that whatever *needs* to be accomplished by the experience may be addressed. This primary directive of the temporal lobes can and often does alter once the scenario is fully under way (e.g., a child, once comforted by an angel, may then ask, "Is that what you really look like?" only to have the angel dissolve into a brilliant burst of light). Experiencers, when so alerted or relaxed, are more likely to go through intense scenarios that foster life-changing characteristics afterward.

Still, accommodations, personal history, what a person has been exposed to during the span of his or her life, even language constraints, do not fully explain all of the contents of near-death states. In *Beyond the Light: What Isn't Being Said About the Near-Death Experience*[16] I described four levels of imagery found in otherworld journeys such as near-death. Briefly, these levels are:

Personal	Images from one's own life.
Mass mind	Images of a collective nature that reflect the human condition.
Memory fields	Primordial, archetypal images that are universal in nature.
Truth	That consistent, stable reality that undergirds and transcends creation and all created things (seldom any imagery per se; rather, a knowing).

(Many authors have written extensively about the imagery in otherworld journeys. I would call your attention to the works of Carl G. Jung, Joseph Campbell, Richard Heinberg, Manley P. Hall, and Ioan Couliano.)[17]

Scenarios can sometimes be better understood if one keeps in mind that subjective imagery has various interpretations. The initial "greeter" is not always who or what it seems to be. The fact remains, however, that the range of details present in the experience places near-death states front and center as a major challenge to anyone's belief that the life we have, and who we think we are, is all there is.

SPIRIT SHIFT

Spirit shifts bespeak a larger agenda, one that transcends personal and societal concerns and expectations, and seems determinant in why some individuals have a brain shift while others do not, even if mutual conditions are similar.

I offer this observation without hesitation, for one cannot research near-death and other transformative states as long as I have without recognizing a greater power at work, as well as a subtle spirit or soul force that appears to be responsible for the outworking of that greater power.

Repeatedly, experiencers describe this subtle presence as a highly organized, intelligent luminosity that plays the role of emissary for the Divine, God, Source, or whatever title one prefers. Apparently, this intelligent luminosity can take on any form or color or substance or odor, yet is always available as a nonenergetic force, a Holy Spirit capable of moving in and through us once we are ready or once we surrender to it.[18] Experiencers claim that should we ignore its presence or remain locked in a particular lifestyle that denies our true purpose or "life mission," this subtle spirit can forcibly intervene, and if it does, a shift occurs.

How this plays out with child experiencers of near-death states is worth a closer look. The depth of maturity that emerges from these youngsters threatens as many people as it inspires. Since spirit shifts lack the physicality of brain shifts, I will rely more in this section on quotes from my case studies to convey the stirring of spirit.

Linda A. Jacquin, Missouri. NDE at age four and a half, drowning. "At a recent meeting I was talking about my childhood near-death experience. A few days later, I received a note from a fellow experiencer who was there. She said she received a message for me from a divine being. The message was: 'A good fisherman practices the catch-and-release philosophy. If the fish he catches is too small, it is simply returned to the water so it can grow some more.' She felt that my brush with death was reviewed and judged by the Divine and that the judgment was to return me to let me grow. I agree. Perhaps this is why children who have near-death experiences are sent back to earth. Like little fishes, they need time for their spirits to grow."

Anell Q. Tubbs, Boise, Idaho. NDE before age eight, blow to head. "I have come to the conclusion *I am normal.* Every person on this planet is here for the same reason—to grow and to learn—and everyone is at a different stage in their evolutionary process. Everyone has the same ability to heal and be psychic and know things. If they don't exhibit these abilities now, they will."

Emily, Seattle, Washington. NDE at age two from high fever; at five from complications during surgery. "I believe in modern society we mistakenly focus primarily upon physical and material needs and neglect our emotions and spirit. I am deeply committed to helping people achieve health in Mind, Soul, and Body through alternative medicine. I sense a change coming and I hope to be part of it in a positive way."

Regina Patrick, Toledo, Ohio. NDE at age four, pneumonia. "My ultimate mission is to have a home, a place where people can come to die, and to do spiritual work with the dying—to help them, strengthen them, and prepare them to go on. I've done hospice work, volunteered at nursing homes through my church. I have a ministry sharing The Journey, which is for people struggling with life-threatening illness."

Joe Ann Van Gelder, Newport, Vermont. Nine NDEs as a child, multiple illnesses and accidents. "My experiences have led me to believe that our human evolution involves the development of a different level of consciousness, which requires our physical bodies to adapt to higher vibratory frequencies. I was told by my guidance to move my geographic location to the forty-fifth parallel, halfway between the equator and the North Pole. When I did, everything improved for me."

Diana Schmidt, El Cerrito, California. NDE at age nine, undiagnosed seizure. "I have discovered the suppressed and forgotten feminine foundations of our culture, and think that the paradigm of the New Age is the Dark Goddess and Sophia—*Light comes from the Dark*. I celebrate and speak whenever I can on this paradigm change and teach a course called 'The Symbolic Life,' which shows people how symbols are a source of renewal and healing. I do this through symbol systems such as tarot, I Ching, astrology, runes, etc."

Christina Moon, Eureka Springs, Arkansas. Two NDEs, complications at birth. "I describe my 'religion' thusly: take a computer card for each of the major religions of the world and stack them up. Mine would be where the holes match and go all the way through. In other words, I have a very eclectic philosophy and would describe myself as a Buddhist

Pagan. I am guided by a concern and a compassion for all living beings no matter what shape, size, or species. I try to live in a way that will add to rather than detract from the world."

Laura, San Francisco, California. NDE at age three and a half, child abuse and during surgery. "I learned how to live with my murderer for another fifteen years by learning what I could from him and leaving the rest. I learned that the most important phenomena in the universe are love, truth, and the quest for knowledge. I received a clear sense of my purpose in life and how I must achieve it. I was given the gift of foreseeing things before they happen and the ability to visualize events, images, and forms, and then bring them into being. I learned that we are wounded, and heal from deep wounds, not so that we may somehow be safe forever, but so that we may be wounded again in a new way. Most of all, I acquired a deep love of death and a longing to be in the presence of God again, a longing that is with me every moment of every day. It is only for the knowledge of His presence that I am able to live."

N.T.A., Omaha, Nebraska. NDE at age thirteen months, electrical shock. "I believe every person is a spiritual being and that we all have a special purpose that is spiritually oriented. I believe we are all light beings of love and that Christ came to teach us that we could be like him. I believe in the concept of unity of all things. I think that the history we have been taught for thousands of years is not the whole truth, and that these truths are coming out. Many earth changes are taking place and many ascended beings [Holy Ones] are helping and guiding us through this time of transition. It is time for us to be okay in questioning our beliefs and to take responsibility in healing ourselves and the planet—to hold more light. I believe 'bad' things, people, and experiences are opportunities for growth. As we awaken and remember, we will begin to create heaven on earth. My near-death experience has made me realize and know without a doubt that love and happiness, acceptance and joy, are possible for every person."

The majority of the child experiencers I interviewed had the gift of conversing directly with spirit afterward. And they spoke of divine intervention as an active force in their lives.

An example of divine intervention is what happened to Stephanie Lang of New York City. She nearly died at the age of three from a severe kidney infection complicated by measles, chicken pox, and a raging fever. Although she does not remember having had a near-death experience per se, she went on to exhibit most of the aftereffects. Along with a sharp mind and incredible artistic talent, she struggled with depression and a lack of motivation, and felt somehow "off course." While lunching one day on the roof of a twenty-six-floor skyscraper, she walked to the railing with the intent of just looking around. She began to rock, absent-mindedly lost her balance, and pitched forward toward the traffic below. Before she could react, she suddenly found herself ten feet back from the railing, sitting on her bottom with tears streaming. A clear voice in her head spoke: "Are you going or are you staying? If you are staying, you have to change." She credits this rescue to divine intervention. It totally changed her life; afterward, she became goal oriented and excited about taking advantage of every opportunity she could. Even though doubts still assail her from time to time, the deep depressions she once had are gone.

This closeness to spirit, a sense of the Divine, of God, propels experiencers into a search for more and better avenues of service, mission, and outreach. Says Tonecia Maxine McMillan of Oxon Hill, Maryland, who at age eleven drowned: "I was mean, self-centered, and egotistical before, but, when my episode was over, I was more peaceful and I really cared about people and wanted to help them." She became a nurse as a result, and has devoted her life to taking care of others' needs.

It is true that many are frustrated by a lack of any clear knowing or message telling them exactly what to do with their lives or how, but just as many are like McMillan—motivated and alive with the faith that where they're headed is the right path for them. Jungian analyst James Hillman addresses this in his book *The Soul's Code: Character, Calling and Fate.*[19] He states, "Psychotherapy has become an exaggerated self-searching to find out who we are but has neglected entirely the search for what the world wants from us—our *calling.*" David Spangler, author of *The Call,*[20] expands on Hillman's idea, saying: "You *are* your own unique self, and if you have the humility to break through the boundaries of ego you will hear the summons of your Call. Something you may not even know about yourself will emerge, and you will discover a service, a gift, a divine purpose behind your actions."

Prayer and meditation take on dynamic proportions immediately following a child's near-death experience, as does *visioning* (aligning in consciousness with the divine purpose within us to love and to express a greater degree of life and caring). Many of these youngsters actually *saw* prayers being said for them while they were out of body. They describe how the power of those prayers turned into beams of radiant, golden, or rainbow light that arced over from the one saying the prayer, no matter how many miles away, to where they themselves were "hovering." Once the prayer beam reached them, the feeling would be akin to a "splash" of love or an incredible warming. Because they have seen and felt the effectiveness of prayer, child experiencers consider it a valid and real way to talk with God while sharing God's healing love with others.

Larry Dossey, M.D., former chief of staff of Humana Medical City in Dallas, Texas, and current cochairman of the panel on mind/body interventions in the Office of Alternative Medicine at the National Institutes of Health, has a lot to say about the power of prayer, both in his books and personally:[21] "There is a quality that correlates with the effect of the prayer, and it's something that sounds very old-fashioned. It's love. And if the individual doing the praying does not have compassion and empathy and love and a deep sense of authentic and genuine caring for whoever they are praying for, these [medical] experiments [on the power of prayer] don't work very well. Love is the key to success."

Typically, children seem obsessed with worship and attending church after their episodes. Barbara True Bradley of Des Moines, Iowa (who "died" at four and a half from lobar pneumonia), said, "When I was well and returned home, I set up a table in my bedroom, covered it with a white cloth, and had a prayer book and cross on it. I remember kneeling there to pray."

Those who had been steeped in certain religious dogmas beforehand, though, ofttimes found the call to express the inner spirit running counter to their earlier indoctrination. To appreciate why child experiencers are more apt than adult experiencers to lose the pure spontaneity and utter joy of their new relationship with God, consider these incidents.

I remember questioning everything the minister and Sunday School teacher said. I became belligerent in Sunday School. I stopped going to choir practice. I used science to prove religion (nothing can be created or destroyed, only changed) and applied it to body/soul.

Judy, New York. NDE at age eleven,
complications during a tonsillectomy

I stood up in class and asked Father Marginen, "How is it you teach that if I stand by and say nothing when someone is doing wrong, I am as guilty as the person doing wrong? Yet you say it was the Jews who crucified Christ, when in truth it was the Romans who drove the nails into His hands and feet and pierced His side. Why are they not guilty?"

Dorothy M. Bernstein, North Olmsted, Ohio.
NDE as a toddler, twice stopped breathing

I was brought up Methodist until I asked the "wrong" questions and was pulled out of church. My parents were told by my Sunday School teacher that I was disrupting the class by asking [questions] about church dogma he could not or would not answer.

Robert C. Warth, Little Silver, New Jersey.
NDE at age five, complications during a tonsillectomy

Child experiencers seldom remain alienated from God if they are ever "turned off," but their feelings about religion and church attendance do change. The split of those who stay in religious settings versus those who choose a more eclectic spiritual path is about the same as with adult experiencers: one-third stay, two-thirds leave. But youngsters are more than twice as likely as adults to cut ties permanently.

(Adult experiencers usually rediscover the value of church with time, and return to a church setting, though rarely the one of their youth. They seem to prefer "new thought" churches like Unity, Religious Science, or Baha'i.)

Kathleen Norris, a published poet and author, speaks to this schism between the church of one's youth and the challenge to make peace with what once seemed so divisive. Although she does not claim to be a near-death experiencer, her behavior traits and memories suggest that she may have had such an episode as an infant. She recalls:

> I didn't do living right, at first. When I was six months old, I nearly died. All wrong, for an infant to be so caught up in the last things. Naturally, the hospital was called Providence; in all likelihood, as I was in danger of dying, a nun baptized me there. My official baptism came four months later, in the arms of my grandfather Norris, a Methodist pastor. Six months of age is too early to learn that one's mother and father are helpless before death. But the struggle that took place in my infant body and still-forming pre-verbal intelligence was between life and death, and I am convinced that a sense of something vast, something yet to come, took hold in my consciousness and remains there still.

In her journey to erase what she felt was religious bigotry, she turned to the arts, revisiting her home church years later only to discover that she liked being there and conversing with the ministers. She eventually joined a monastery and immersed herself in Christianity. After becoming a lay minister, she shared what she learned about religion and the spiritual quest in two books, *The Cloister Walk* and *Amazing Grace*.[22]

While religion is a systematized approach to spiritual development formed around set standards or dogmas, spirituality emerges from a personal, intimate experience of God. There are no standards or dogmas, only precedents, as individual knowing or gnosis is honored. Needlessly at odds with each other, both routes to a more positive, uplifting, and meaningful life are equally valid and worthy.

Ken Wilber, author of *A Brief History of Everything*,[23] puts this issue into perspective by describing it in evolutionary terms: "Consciousness evolution moves from prepersonal to personal to transpersonal; from subconscious to self-conscious to superconscious; from premental to mental to supramental; from instinct to ego to God."

An integral part of spirit shifts is the flowering of psychic abilities. This rankles more people and causes more misunderstandings than any other aspect of the phenomenon. Few can adequately address why this occurs. Cries of "It's the devil's work" are as commonplace as "This is God's gift." Here are some incidents of this nature as reported by child experiencers in my study:

Gracie L. Sprouse, Keene, Virginia. NDE at age eleven, drowning. "I believed myself to be psychic until I learned that psychic abilities may be from Satan. Yet constant, instant miracles have never ceased in my life; they have in fact increased. The more I recognize them, the more they happen. I now believe these to be Godly abilities."

P. Bradley Carey, Burlington, Washington. NDE at age thirteen, choked by boy at school. "I heard the radio playing when the dial indicated it wasn't. Then what sounded like a commercial started. In it, the company gave their telephone number, which I wrote down figuring to prove to myself that it was just my imagination. I dialed it. A ceramic store clerk answered (located in Spokane, on the other side of the state). After asking a few questions, I found out that their commercial was only being carried in their locality. There are so many miles and mountains between us that the signal can't get down here. It was totally impossible for me to hear this ad. I live in the middle of nowhere, no traffic, no neighbors, and there was no radio on. How did I hear the radio commercial?"

Cecil L. Hamilton, Palmyra, Virginia. NDE at age eleven, drowning. "How do you use the information you have? I see so many psychic fakes. I can tell where their experience ends and guesswork begins. I know the future, especially with little, ongoing things. I know when people are about to die. I try sometimes to turn it off—'cause you don't enjoy going out to dinner and seeing death on someone at the table."

Rhona Alterman-Newman, Cherry Hill, New Jersey. NDE at age six months, strangulated hernia. "Ten days after my mother died, she came back to her room and checked to see if we'd turned off the heating pad. The reason I think she did this is because, when we left for the hospital with her, we left the pad on and she was concerned about that. It scared me to see her that night. I was fully awake when she came."

Francis Piekarski, New Martinsville, West Virginia. NDE at age five, drowning, and at twelve, high fever, bone infection. "Perhaps the craziest thing that happened was when I was listening to JFK politicking in Charleston. I wanted to stand up with him onstage and tell him things that I knew about him. I could have changed his future, but I didn't. This has happened several times, like a time warp. The single greatest change my episodes gave me is an unwavering *knowing* that I had seen God and that I have two angels watching over me."

Lynn, Michigan. NDE at age thirteen, during open-heart surgery. "I know things about people. I have become very psychic. I find people react to this in different ways. Some want to be your 'friend' and then ask you questions all the time—about boyfriends, lottery numbers, interpersonal relationships. This type of 'friend' is a user. Some have accused me of being a witch. They confuse being psychic with witchcraft and devil worship. These are usually 'born again,' and they either want to 'save' me or kill me. Others hear about me and believe I can work miracles. It's amazing what this group thinks I can do. I have been credited with healing people, healing relationships, and uncrossing any situation a person might find themselves in. One woman went so far as to climb through my open bedroom window and sit on my bed one night, asking me to bring her husband back to her. I was only sixteen. I screamed when this woman touched my hand. My mother got her to leave."

Lauren Thibodean, Madison, Ohio. NDE at age six, electrocuted. "I became very psychic, although I'd already shown signs prior to my near-death experience. My childhood was lonely; I was nicknamed 'Jinx' and 'Witch Girl.' Some parents in the neighborhood would not let their children play with me or come to our house. I've had ongoing, very positive 'visits' from beings made of light, which I think of as the angels who rescued me when I was electrocuted, and past-life recall."

Carroll Gray, Atlanta, Georgia. One prebirth experience, five NDEs in childhood, mostly from child abuse injuries. "I have some precognition, like knowing who is on the phone before picking up, or knowing when Mother wants to be called. I see auras. There have also been several instances of telekinesis; I once tossed a child about fifteen feet backward from across the yard simply by 'thinking' it so. This surprised me, frightened my mother, and the child I tossed never came back to play with me again."

Clara Lane, Belmont, Ohio. NDE at age ten, complications during surgery for acute appendicitis. "Many times I have awakened in the middle of the night to see people standing in my bedroom and in the hallway. They turn to look at me, then vanish. I do not feel afraid. Several times we have lived in houses that were haunted. I could sense things. Seeing people in my bedroom at night still happens to me thirty-eight years later. I believe they are watching over me all the time, but only at night do they become visible."

Child experiencers often speak about the light they saw surrounding living things while they were out of their bodies. They claim this light was as beautiful as prayer beams, and seemed to consist of a similar energy. Many, like Carroll Gray, continue to see this light or aura on an ongoing basis.

It can be a real challenge for youngsters to handle a phenomenon such as this, or, for that matter, any of the faculty extensions that typically occur. An excellent book for introducing kids to the psychic realities of near-death states is Kathleen J. Forti's *The Door to the Secret City*.[24] Forti had a near-death episode in her late teens, described in my book *Future Memory,* that accurately presaged events in her adult life, including being a storyteller for children.

The flowering of psychic abilities after a brain shift/spirit shift seems to be more of an enhancement of the limbic system than anything mysterious or paranormal. As such, it relates directly to perceptual enlargements of the electro-magnetic range and to extensions of faculties normal to us. Although an issue for experiencers, the subject touches us all.

It is possible to extend and broaden our five faculties of sight, hearing, touch, taste, and smell to embrace *psychic dimensions* (those beyond reliance on physical forms), and *collective/spiritual realms* (the larger view, grander realities). Since the average person is only aware of 1 percent of what goes on around him or her, these extensions are advantageous and enriching, enabling us to circumvent whatever factors may seem to limit the information we can access. Faculty extensions of this kind are not esoteric, but practical and easily learned by *anyone* with the will to try.

The following chart clarifies what I mean by faculty extensions. Notice what happens to *intuition* and *perception* once our faculties extend and broaden to reach the range of spiritual realities.

Faculty Extensions

Physical Faculty	Psychic Extension	Collective and/or Spiritual Extension
See/Sight	See without use of eyes; research term: "clairvoyance"	Vision
Hear/Sound	Hear without presence of sound; research term: "clairaudience"	Music
Feel/Touch	Feel, or have an effect on an object, without touching; research term: "psychokinesis"	Art
Taste/Flavor	Taste without use of tastebuds; research term: "clairgustation"	Discrimination

Continued

Physical Faculty	Psychic Extension	Collective and/or Spiritual Extension
Smell/Scent	Smell without use of nose; research term: "clairolfaction"	Integrity
Sense/Intuition	Sensing without or in advance of recognition; research term: "clairsentience"	Grace
Perceive/ Perception	Apprehending without or in advance of physical stimuli; research term: "precognition"	Knowing

The root of the word "psychic" means "of the soul." We might infer from this that psychic abilities are really soul abilities, part of our inheritance as children of God—our wellspring of wisdom from within. As with everything else in life, *use determines value.*

Henry Reed, Ph.D., after years of innovative experimentation, found that psychic abilities center around the traits of intimacy and closeness, the bond we share in spirit. The workshops he now gives, called The Intuitive Heart, and his paper titled "Intimacy and Psi: Explorations in Psychic Closeness" are based on this fresh new approach.[25] He explains: "Communicating heart to heart is another way of knowing; the way of intuition, and intuition is the key to the twenty-first century. The consciousness revolution has discovered the psychic outside the brain, not within it. The intuitive heart is visionary, psychic, it has soul, and its essence is spiritual. Developing access to intuition is not a mental trick; it is a matter of caring."

The word "heaven" comes from the Greek language. In the language of the Bible, which is Aramaic, the word was often interchanged with the word "leaven." Jesus is quoted in Matthew 13:33 as saying, "The kingdom of heaven is like unto leaven." Leaven causes dough to rise. Leaven expands, yet the Greeks understood that heaven is *that which is already expanded*. With that clue from the Greek version of what heaven might be, allow me to conjecture. *Brain shift/spirit shift* may well function as does leaven, expanding the consciousness and faculties of the experiencer into the next phase of growth and learning. Individual consciousness once expanded could extend to and connect with other dimensions of reality and higher levels of consciousness—perhaps mass mind or even the One Mind. Having expanded in this manner, the person's consciousness could become *greater than before,* perhaps permanently . . . a true shift.

THREE

A NEW VIEW
OF NEAR-DEATH
STATES

I believe there are two sides to the phenomenon known as death, this side where we live, and the other side where we shall continue to live. Eternity does not start with death. We are in eternity now.

Norman Vincent Peale

On average, near-death experiencers are without pulse or breath for about ten to fifteen minutes. It is not uncommon to hear of individuals being dead for an hour or more; some "wake up" in the morgue. The same is true with children. Since the brain can be permanently damaged in three to five minutes without sufficient oxygen, it is important to note that one of the striking features of the near-death phenomenon is that *no matter how long the person is dead, there is usually no brain damage once he or she is revived; rather, there is a noticeable brain enhancement.*

Because this is true, near-death states provide a dynamic lens through which we can continue to explore the many aspects of brain shift/spirit shift and what such a transformation of consciousness implies.

The term "near-death experience" was coined by Raymond A. Moody, Jr., M.D., in his 1975 book *Life After Life,*[1] to describe the anomaly of resuscitated patients who reported life on the other side of death. Five years later, Kenneth Ring scientifically verified Moody's work in *Life at Death.*[2] These two books legitimized the plethora of research papers, other books, articles, and speculations that followed—all of them based on the same model of eight basic scenario components.

These components are:

1. *A sensation of floating out of one's body,* often followed by an out-of-body experience in which all that goes on around the "vacated" body is both seen and heard.
2. *Passing through a dark tunnel or black space,* accompanied by a feeling or sensation of acceleration—wind may be heard or felt.
3. *Ascending toward a light of incredible brilliance that emits loving peacefulness,* with the possibility of seeing deceased relatives, animals, plants, scenery, and cities.
4. *Being greeted by friendly voices, loved ones, and/or beings made of light.* Conversation can ensue, and a message may be given.
5. *Seeing a panoramic review of the life just lived,* from birth to death or in reverse order, sometimes a reliving rather than a dispassionate viewing.
6. *A different sense of time and space;* the discovery that time and space do not exist.
7. *A reluctance to return to the earthplane,* but a feeling of obligation to so a job can be finished or a mission performed.
8. *Disappointment at being revived,* even anger or tearfulness at being back.

Few near-death episodes include all eight components. Most encompass about five. This confuses people who may have had such an experience and has given rise to a major complaint voiced by those who attend local meetings of the International Association for Near-Death Studies (IANDS) through any of its Friends of IANDS affiliates in the United States, Canada, and around the world.[3] The complaint? *What happened to them doesn't match the "classical" model.*

Since this discrepancy involves so many people and happens so often, the time has come to admit how the original model came into being. *It is a composite of elements common to the experience that was created by the media to sensationalize Moody's first book.* My work differs because I was never privy to what others in the newly emerging field were doing, nor was I influenced by the press.

Right off, I isolated *four* distinctive types of near-death experiences. I discovered elements similar to those described by Moody and Ring but different patterning from what was billed as the classical version; each pattern type was accompanied by a subtle psychological profile suggestive of other forces that might be present. These four types have consistently held up throughout two decades of interviews, observations, and analysis regardless of a person's age, education, gender, culture, or religion. In *Beyond the Light* I used separate chapters to discuss each of the four types. What I offer here is a shorter rendition of the scenario patterns. Children's cases follow as illustrative examples of each type.

The Four Types of Near-Death Experiences

Initial Experience (sometimes referred to as the "nonexperience")
Involves elements such as a loving nothingness, the living dark, a friendly voice, or a brief out-of-body episode. Usually experienced by those who seem to need the least amount of evidence for proof of

survival, or who need the least amount of shakeup in their lives at that point in time. Often, this becomes a "seed" experience or an introduction to other ways of perceiving and recognizing reality.

Incident rate: 76% with child experiencers
20% with adult experiencers

Unpleasant or Hell-like Experience (inner cleansing and self-confrontation)
Encounter with a threatening void or stark limbo or hellish purgatory, or scenes of a startling and unexpected indifference, even "hauntings" from one's own past. Usually experienced by those who seem to have deeply suppressed or repressed guilts, fears, and angers and/or those who expect some kind of punishment or discomfort after death.

Incident rate: 3% with child experiencers
15% with adult experiencers

Pleasant or Heaven-like Experience (reassurance and self-validation)
Heaven-like scenarios of loving family reunions with those who have died previously, reassuring religious figures or light beings, validation that life counts, affirmative and inspiring dialogue. Usually experienced by those who most need to know how loved they are and how important life is and how every effort has a purpose in the overall scheme of things.

Incident rate: 19% with child experiencers
47% with adult experiencers

Transcendent Experience (expansive revelations, alternate realities)
Exposure to otherworldly dimensions and scenes beyond the individual's frame of reference; sometimes includes revelations of greater truths. Seldom personal in content. Usually experienced by those who are ready for a mind-stretching challenge and/or individuals who are more apt to utilize (to whatever degree) the truths that are revealed to them.

Incident rate: 2% with child experiencers
18% with adult experiencers

Note: I have noticed that all four types can occur during the same experience for the same person at the same time, can exist in varying combinations, or can spread out across a series of episodes for a particular individual. Generally speaking, however, each represents a distinctive type of experience occurring but once to a given person.

INITIAL EXPERIENCE

Sophia Carmien, Boulder, Colorado. NDE at age four. "I was swimming in a neighborhood swimming pool. There were two lifeguards. Mom sat me down near the pool and went to the dressing room to change. She said, 'Don't jump in the deep pool without water wings.' I had no water wings on but I thought I did. So, I jumped. Part of me was down below splashing around, not able to see much. The other part was floating up, way up higher than the lifeguards. I heard something behind me, all around me, 'speak' an unspoken question: 'Do you want to live?' I thought about that. Dying seemed somehow good, nice. Dying feels normal. And then I thought about my parents and how sad they would be. Even though it seemed nice to go, I said, 'I'll stay.' I slowly went back down in the water to the other half of me. The next thing I knew I was being held by a fat lady in a polka-dot bathing suit. I thanked her for helping me. Afterward, I thought it was normal, being as young as I was, for this kind of thing to happen to everyone."

Joe Ann Van Gelder, Newport, Vermont. Nine NDEs from age fifteen months to age ten. "My first eleven years found me challenged with both chronic and acute illnesses, including polio, plus various serious accidents. The next five years found me on a slow recovery. During each of my childhood near-death experiences I encountered a warm, supportive darkness, almost womblike, which communicated a sense of love and safety to me. This friendly darkness was not a scary place; neither was it a 'void.' It was indescribable, timeless, spaceless— where the 'real I' goes. I had many aftereffects, increasing in intensity after each experience. As a child, I took my near-death episodes as natural and normal because my mother had

had such an experience as a young adult. There was no reason for me to feel strange or weird since she understood."

UNPLEASANT OR HELL-LIKE EXPERIENCE

Diana Schmidt, El Cerrito, California. NDE at age nine. "It is
high noon and I am in the 'chopped' (weed-free) backyard
of my paternal grandfather. I see my nine-year-old self walk
across the yard and put my head down on a tree stump. A
giant ax appears and splits my head open. What falls out
onto the ground rather than brains are crawling, wiggling
maggots! This was a terrible experience for me. It wiped out
any good feelings I had about myself, as I thought I was
filled with something repugnant. This 'dream' left me feeling totally frightened and ashamed. After being operated on
at twenty-nine for the removal of a blood clot in my brain,
I remember being so relieved. It was good news! I had a
brain, not a skull full of maggots. Considering my history of
blood clots and seizures, I believe this incident was an undiagnosed seizure resulting from a congenital or inherited
angioma [swelling or tumor]."

Adrianna Norton, Modesto, California. NDE at age five. "I was
born with a large hole in my heart, which wasn't fixed sur-
gically until I was an adult. When I was five, I was stricken
with the flu and a very high fever. During the night I
found myself up in the corner of the ceiling looking down
at my small sleeping body. Suddenly, I was floating in a
black cube about twelve feet square with black matter,
black clawlike hands everywhere and clawing at me. I was
horrified; there was no opening for escape. Again suddenly,
I was floating facedown in a 'sea' of opalescent light and

felt the most warm, safe, secure, loved, comforting feeling. Waves of light tenderly massaged me. Then I was back in my body and back on the bed, exhausted. My fever was gone and I fell asleep. I thought it was a nightmare and tried to forget it. I could not. I tried to repress the memory of it *because the frightening episode overwhelmed the pleasant one,* yet it has remained vivid all my life. I've been claustrophobic ever since."

PLEASANT OR HEAVEN-LIKE EXPERIENCE

Gracie L. Sprouse, Keene, Virginia. NDE at age eleven. "I was swimming with my sisters when suddenly I found myself unable to reach the top of the water for air. It felt like I had just stepped into nothingness. I went down twice and was coming up for the third time when I managed to yell for help. Before I was pulled from the water, I saw a filmstrip of my life. It was just like being in a theater, as I sat cross-legged and watched the things I'd done wrong to my sisters. I was

not judged by the angel who showed me this; I judged and convicted myself. The angel hovered in midair, to the upper left of the screen. I remember thinking that I was leaving my family and sisters and started to feel sorrow. The sorrow left immediately and I felt as if I'd been assured they would be fine. Then, there was such a feeling of bliss that it's indescribable. Since then, I have had a lifetime of unexplained happenings. My entire outlook is different from the norm. *I see with my heart.*"

Clara Lane, Belmont, Ohio. NDE at age ten. "I was in the fifth grade when I became sick with extreme pain in my lower right side. My teacher thought it was only a stomachache and ignored it. Two hours later I was rushed to the hospital. I was terrified and begged to go home. I was fighting the ether mask when it happened. One second I was awake, scared to death, the next second I was falling straight down a dark hole as if in a well. There were loud sounds like buzzing and ringing and metal scraping together, then I was up by the ceiling looking down on myself. I felt as though I was spread out all over the room like vapor or a cloud. I

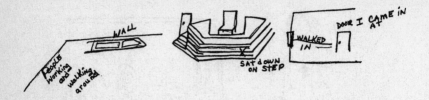

watched as the doctor had a square green machine wheeled into the room by a nurse, and then worked on me using it. There were several nurses there. Suddenly I was standing alone in a room with large, heavy doors leading into other rooms. Someone came to me. I didn't see him; I only heard his voice. He led me up through what seemed like a tunnel. I seemed to be walking, but my feet didn't touch a floor. Suddenly I heard what sounded like a city-sized playground full of kids, laughing and playing. Hearing them calmed me. Another man came to meet us. I didn't see him either. He asked the one leading me who I was, then he went away. When he returned he told the man with me that I had to go back, that they weren't ready for me yet. I was led up a sidewalk to a large building with large doors. I walked inside and saw people all around working and doing things. I was taken to a huge iridescent white room and told to sit down on some steps that led up to a large white chair, and wait there for someone who was to talk to me. He came out a door at the other end of the steps, walked to the chair above me, and sat down. He was dressed in a white, long-sleeved, floor-length robe with a wide gold band around the mid-section. He wore sandals. His dark brown hair was shoulder length; he had a long face, broad chin, dark eyes with black around both eyelids, like eyeliner pencil, but it wasn't. His skin was olive colored and his eyes were as liquid love. He communicated by looking at me. No words had to be spoken, as we could hear each other's thoughts. He told me what I had to do in life and had me go to the other side of the room and look down into something like a TV set so I could see my future. What I saw made me very happy. This man, who I believe is Jesus Christ, said that once I woke up in the hospital I would forget what I was supposed to do in life. 'Nothing can happen before its time,' He cautioned. As I was leaving the room He said I must obey His commandments if I wanted to come back. When I revived, a nurse was sitting beside my bed and she said, 'Thank God you finally woke up.' I told the doctor that I had watched him work on me and the color of the machine brought into the surgery room. He didn't know what to say."

TRANSCENDENT EXPERIENCE

Cecil L. Hamilton, Palmyra, Virginia. NDE at age eleven. "My brother and I went swimming. He had a problem. I tried to get him out of the water, but in his panic he pulled me under several times. We both drowned. He died and I came back. I can remember it all like yesterday. Just as I could no longer stay afloat, a strange sound like ringing in my ears started. A peaceful feeling came over me. I felt my spirit come out of my body and I went into a black void. That was a little frightening. A long way off there was a pinprick of light. I moved toward it, slowly at first, then faster and faster as if I were on top of a train accelerating. Then I stopped and stepped fully into the light. I noticed everything—sky, buildings, glass—emitted its *own* light. And everything was much more colorful than what we see here. A river meandered around. On the other side was a city, and a road running through it to another city, and another city, and another and another. Right in front of me but across the river were three men. They projected themselves to me. They didn't walk or fly; they projected over. I didn't recognize them, yet I knew one was Lynn Bibb. (I was named after him. He died a matter of weeks before I was born.) I knew these three men were looking out for me, like a welcoming committee to escort me over the river to the first city. I had the feeling that if I went with them, there would be no coming back, so I hesitated. The first city was like first grade. People stayed there until they were ready to go to the next city—your eternal progression, from city to city. Behind me and to the left was a strong light source, very brilliant and filled with love. I knew it was a person. I called it God for lack of a better term. I could not see it; I felt what seemed like a male presence. He communicated to me, not so much in words but telepathically, and he asked, 'Why did you hesitate?' I replied, 'Well, I'm kind of young to die.' He chuckled. 'We have babies die.' I said, 'Well, there's some things I want to know first.' He replied, 'What do you want to know?' 'What is death?' I asked. He said, 'Turn and look to one side.' As I did, I saw a bad car wreck. Several people had been killed. Out of some of the bodies a spirit came up to progress on. Some who did not believe it was possible stayed in their bodies and would not emerge. I asked if they could be reached and he said, 'Yes, some more quickly than others and some maybe never.' Death, then, is not believing in anything. I asked, 'What is hell?' He said, 'Turn and look again.' I saw an old woman in a rocking chair determined to sit and rock and worry about children and grandchildren and everything else. Hell is therefore a lack of wisdom and not moving on, choosing not to go any further, sitting there and doing nothing. Hell is not a place. I asked if there was a Devil or Satan. He said to me, 'Would God allow that?' He continued, 'If I made you God for just a few seconds, what would you do first?' I knew my first act would be to eliminate any Devil or Satan. I asked, 'How do I know right from wrong?' He replied, 'Right is helping and being kind. Wrong is not only hurting someone but not helping when you can.' We walked as I asked about the universe and reasons for everything. All of these things were shown to me. Then he wondered if I still wanted to return to the physical world. 'I do want to return.' He asked, 'Why?' I said I would help my mother whom my father had left with four children and one on the way. God kind of chuckled and asked me for the real reason. I said I would leave the earth a little better than I found it. 'Then you may return with some of the knowledge of the things you have learned, but the rest will be veiled for a time. Live in such a way that you will not feel bad when you return here again.' I woke up facedown in the mud of the river bottom and was 'lifted' to the top. I threw up great amounts of water, then pulled myself out of the river only to discover that my brother had died."

The vast majority of youngsters have Initial Experiences, and those Initial Experiences can involve powerful *feelings, knowings,* and often *a sense of presence,* which greatly affect the child and leave a lasting impression. For instance, the warm and friendly dark experienced especially by the young is incredibly important. This darkness is similar to that of the womb, a protective love cradle, yet it somehow "voices" instructions and enjoys lively dialogue. Unlike the womb, it is *the Darkness That Knows.*

In direct contrast to adult cases, imagery is not necessarily a prime component of children's near-death episodes, nor is light.

And the dark that little ones experience should not be confused with tunnels. Yes, kids do describe tunnels on occasion, but not nearly as often as do older experiencers. Even among adults the tunnel component to the scenario is not that common. I have encountered this so-called stereotypical element among less than 30 percent of those I have interviewed. In the original Gallup poll, conducted in 1982, only 9 percent mentioned a tunnel. Many times I've actually seen adults change their near-death accounts to include a tunnel so they could fit in and avoid the embarrassment of not matching the "classical" model.

The life review of the very young commonly consists of vivid prebirth scenarios and past-life remembrances, recounted, curiously, from the viewpoint of a seemingly "mature mind." A judgmentlike appraisal of the present life from a child's perspective usually doesn't begin until about kindergarten age.

Multiple experiences are as common among kids as they are among adults. The forty-four child experiencers who filled out the questionnaire recorded sixty-one episodes, with 27 percent experiencing another near-death event in adulthood. Van Gelder, who suffered from chronic illness, polio, surgery, and several serious accidents as a child, reported nine events between the ages of fifteen months and ten years, as already noted. Another individual had five as a child and five as an adult, as well as a prenatal memory that was verified by her mother. The record holder in my research base is a man who claimed a total of twenty-three near-death experiences throughout his lifetime, beginning shortly after birth. The man, who asked to remain anonymous, came into the world with severe physical handicaps and was not expected to live. He was in his late forties when I interviewed him. After countless surgeries, he felt he never could have survived as long as he had without the healing strength he gained from each near-death episode.

Drowning was by far the most frequent cause of death among the children in my study. Large numbers also "died" from suffocation; during or after major surgery or during tonsillectomies; and from child abuse (in that order). Other traumas were described, like those from high fever and being hit by lightning, but what captures my attention are the tonsillectomies—a minor operation that has hardly garnered a single headline in modern medicine.

Consider what happened to Robert C. Warth of Little Silver, New Jersey, when he was five. His mother and father took him to a local doctor's office to have his tonsils out. Three other children were already there, sitting on beds with their pajamas on. He was ushered to the fourth bed. Soon after his mother told him that the doctor was going to remove something from his throat, a nurse came and took him to another room where the doctor was. She put a mask over his face. "It dripped something sickeningly sweet," he recalled. Instantly he found himself above the domed operating light looking down, and was surprised to see his body below him along with a layer of dust atop the light fixture. "I could see 360 degrees without moving," he noted. Fighting back tears, he described a scene that still horrifies him. "My mouth was pried open and I was covered up to my neck. There was a frenzy. The nurse yelled, 'Doctor.' He swung around and said, 'Stand back.' The next thing I remember is waking up in the bed, and I couldn't talk and I felt miserable." Two weeks later Robert was taken back to the doctor for a checkup. He described for the doctor everything he had seen and heard. "The doctor winked at my mother and said, 'They tell me stories often. It's the ether. It makes them dream and hallucinate.' What else was the doctor going to say, that the little creep stopped breathing? I saw what he did, and he couldn't get me out of his office fast enough."

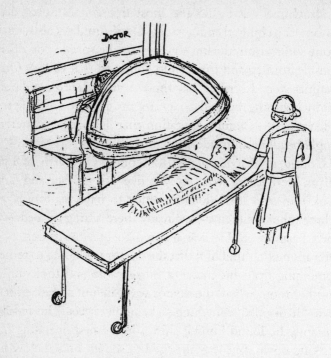

Melvin Morse, M.D., in his seminal work with children, noted that during the early to mid-1900s doctors regularly used too much ether for tonsillectomies, and that's why so many show up in near-death cases during that period. This practice changed by the late seventies (although cases like this are still reported). Apparently, *excessive* amounts of ether can trigger near-death states with some children instead of the simple hallucinations many report. My research caught the same "error of judgment" regarding the drug that Morse did, verifying his findings, but I also discovered something else. *Medical mistakes readily surface in near-death scenarios.* They may be individual incidents as when the patient while out of body witnesses what the doctor or nurse really did; or they may show up as an unusual percentage of people "dying" from a nonthreatening procedure, as in the case of children across the country being overdosed with ether during tonsillectomies. The accuracy of these reports suggests that the range of human faculties is as nonlocal as the mind—something the medical community would be wise to note.

Over 70 percent of children's near-death scenarios involve angel visitations. Small children are not as explicit in their descriptions as older kids, yet the majority describe the angels as winged and either bright or dark or colored "like real folks are." The very young seldom use the term "angel"; rather, they speak of "the people" or describe loving beings made of light.

Youngsters are also met by:

- *Deceased relatives and friends,* always authentic and genuine even if unknown to the child at the time. Invariably, these are later verified.
- *Animals and deceased pets,* along with sensations of being licked, rubbed, pawed, or nosed by the animal. Critters sometimes converse telepathically or serve as guides. Occasionally, kids report having to visit the animal heaven before they can go to the heaven where people are.
- *Religious figures,* described as being more wonderful than angels. Many children were exposed to Christianity before their experiences and called this "extra special being" Jesus or Christ. Kids of other backgrounds used terms typical of their family of origin, *except* that Jesus and Mohammed were always described as having brown skin and Buddha somewhat yellowish skin, *regardless* of the child's race or culture.
- *God,* experienced as the greatest of fathers or grandfathers (always male, never female) by the very young. Yet

kids school age and above usually saw God as a sphere of all-knowing light.

- *People very much alive,* a rarity, usually involved a favorite teacher or playmate. "Image" lasted only long enough to calm the child, then it disappeared, replaced by more common otherworldly beings such as angels.

To understand children's cases, we must keep in mind that kids are tuned to different harmonics than adults. Concepts of life and death leave them with puzzled faces. "I don't end or begin anywhere," a youngster once told me. "I just reach out and catch the next wave that goes by and hop a ride. That's how I got here."

This child, like other young experiencers, speaks in the language of "other worlds," one that is less verbal and more akin to synesthesia (multiple sensing). This ability enables them to perceive what we call reality as consisting of *layered realms* unrestricted by physical boundaries. Thus, they easily giggle with angels, play with ghosts, and see the future. Parents generally find such behavior cause for panic. Yet what seems worrisome may well have a simple explanation: near-death states expand faculties normal to us, hence allowing access to more of the electromagnetic spectrum.

A fascinating aspect of this is that as a child's mind begins to shift, his or her intelligence increases. Using questionnaire responses, let's take a look at what I'm implying.

Faculties enhanced, altered, or experienced in multiples	77%
Mind works differently—highly creative and inventive	84%
Significant enhancement of intellect	68%

Mind tested at genius level (no genetic markers
  for increase)

main group, overall figure	48%
subgroup, under 6 years	81%

Drawn to and highly proficient in math/science/
  history   93%

Professionally employed in math/science/
  history careers   25%

Unusually gifted with languages   35%

School

easier after experience	34%
harder afterward or blocked from memory	66%

Note: I found no difference between males and females with regard to enhanced intelligence and spatial and mathematical abilities. Although the percentages shown are based on the questionnaire results, they reflect what I have consistently observed with the 277 child experiencers in my study. The lone exception is professional employment. In the larger group, the figure is 40%, not 25% as shown here, which is still substantially lower than interest level and proficiency.

These figures come close to matching what I have encountered in the average child experiencer since 1978. But I want to make another observation: *after a near-death experience, a child's learning ability reverses; instead of continuing on along the normal developmental curve, from concrete (details) to abstract (concepts), a child returns immersed in broad conceptual reasoning styles and has to learn how to go from abstract back to concrete.*

The most often repeated phrase was: "I felt like an adult in a child's body."

Here are some comments from the experiencers themselves about what it was like for them to grow up this way.

Kenneth S. Taylor, Midlothian, Virginia. NDE at age seven, drowning. "I had a lust for knowledge afterward. By the time I was eight or nine I was reading adult books. I still read a lot and have a large library. The military tested me and discovered I have an unusually high and sharp degree of hearing. I never thought about it before, but they were impressed."

Judith Werner, Bronx, New York. NDE at age nine, during surgery for infection. "I was first in my class through grade school, thirteenth out of a class of one thousand in high school, Phi Beta Kappa and magna cum laude in college. Other people have always seen me as serious, precocious, [focused] inward, stubborn, and a little depressed. I was probably always psychic about the future, but it took many years to admit it to myself."

Susan Firth, Free Union, Virginia. NDE at age two from an accident, at six from drowning. "School was very difficult. From the first day, I experienced negativity in the vibrational airwaves. The sounds, clamor, and noise were dysfunctional to me, and I had to separate [from my body] for safety. I had trouble reading and comprehending, transposing letters, numbers, words. At home the 'broken' record was: 'Won't you ever learn? What are we going to do with you? You are so stupid. Go to your room and don't come out 'til you've learned something.' Consequently, I spent more time [projecting myself] in the tree outside the classroom window with the birds than at the desk where I sat. I was quite adept at being in two places at once."

Beverly A. Brodsky, Philadelphia, Pennsylvania. NDE at age seven and a half, during tonsillectomy. "I was brilliant in school and loved to learn. I read the encyclopedia from cover to cover, first the children's edition, then the adult *World Book*. I devoured books that were supposed to be far above my level. I was accused of plagiarism in the third grade by my English teacher, for spicing up an assignment with an analogy to a Greek myth. I finally convinced her it was my own work. She was stunned. I closed down to everyone except my sister and one friend. I often thought I had an inferiority/superiority complex; inferior because some connection was missing inside me, yet I was so smart I was intellectually superior to my peers."

Robert C. Warth, Little Silver, New Jersey. NDE at age five, during tonsillectomy. "I couldn't stand school. The teacher called in my mother and told her, 'Robert doesn't seem to be able to do the work. I'll have to put him back in kindergarten.' My mother was devastated. She talked to me. I don't know what happened, but within a week I was doing what the second graders were doing and so was able to skip the first grade. By the time I went to another school to finish the sixth grade, I had a miserable reputation with teachers for being the class clown. My teacher hated my guts and told my mother I shouldn't be in the sixth grade. I was sent to a psychiatrist. He said I should be skipped into the seventh grade, but my mother said no. All this time, I was frantically clipping out science articles from every paper I read. Also, I was getting precise dates when things would happen, sometimes years in advance, and I would write them down. They just 'came' to me. I was never sick or late for school in twelve years. Graduated high school with the Bausch and Lomb Science Award for top science students."

Christina Moon, Eureka Springs, Arkansas. Two NDEs, complications at birth. "I am smart. Throughout school I was told that

I have a high IQ. Learning has always come easily to me. My pattern as an adult has been to get interested in something, immerse myself in it until I have learned everything I could about the subject, and then move on to something else. To some this looks like fickle behavior. To me, it is an indication of how interesting things are. I am *never* bored. I don't think linearly. I think in images, feelings, impulses. I sense things."

Carroll Gray, Atlanta, Georgia. Five NDEs due to injuries from child abuse; one prenatal experience. "My father, who had left school at thirteen, was openly threatened by an intelligent, precocious child. Other relatives were very proud but bewildered, as there was no one else in the family like me. By two and a half I could read and write, had a library card, and was reading the newspaper. Had an immediate interest in theater; saw an opera. Read *Hamlet* with some comprehension, and was performing Shakespeare by the age of five. Learned how to fence and have had a real love of good blades and fine swords since after my fourth near-death episode. Began writing poetry at three, plays shortly thereafter. I believe my intelligence level has changed after every episode, though I can't say how. I rarely forget research, names, dates, history, but often can't remember if I've eaten or slept in the past few days. At fourteen, I tested at an IQ of 186. I have no idea what my IQ is after five additional near-death states in adulthood. I don't feel that smart, but over and over people keep telling me I am, almost to the point where they can't converse with me or understand what I'm saying. I, on the other hand, feel that I'm being perfectly clear and simple, and that anyone should be able to grasp what I'm saying."

L. S. Gordon, United States; NDE at age three, during tonsillectomy. "Suddenly began to read right after my near-death experience. Evidenced high IQ. Could think and read at incredible speed. Could think multiple trains of thought. It made a big impression on others that I could read so suddenly and without explanation. When I learned of [Einstein's formula] E = MC squared, I understood that the 'speed of light' was *home*—no time and infinite mass! I got it! I was dismayed that I couldn't get back to 'home.' Read physics and grasped it, even as a ten-year-old. Studied world religions and spiritual practices. Knew that 'earth school' was a Scotch tape–and–cardboard affair. *Always* in trouble, but high IQ won me tolerance. I hated, hated, hated school—skipped, forged notes. Did my reading out in the fields. Without parents initiating the idea, I *knew* I was going to college, and I *knew* I was supposed to. From college on, I was always on the dean's list."

Lauren Thibodean, Madison, Ohio. NDE at age six, electrocuted. "I seem to pick things up very easily. Great facility with languages and math. Honor student throughout school, tested high IQ. Very sensitive to smells and tastes. Unable to tolerate light for long periods. Hypersensitive to sound. My body temperature routinely is about 97 to 97.4 degrees Fahrenheit, blood pressure lower than normal. Often allergic to medications. Animals and nature 'speak' to me."

Carl Allen Pierson, Hinton, West Virginia. NDE before age nine, struck by lightning. "I was an exceptionally bright child. School was a breeze for me. Made straight A's. I have had 20/10 vision; extremely sensitive taste buds—can taste something and usually tell what all the ingredients are and then can cook it. My IQ was 138 in high school. Took another IQ test in the early nineties and my score had gone up to 150."

Anthony Chipoletti, Arnold, Pennsylvania. NDE at age seven during and after tonsillectomy. "I was confident that I could predict the future, such as humans going to the moon, cures for mental and physical illnesses. I can recall saying to count-less people, 'Boredom doesn't exist.' In high school, my classmates and even the chemistry teacher 'gave up' and let me teach the class—at least for a day. I became aware of a *massive* amount of scientific knowledge, specifically chemistry, without any previous studies in science."

These quotes richly illustrate the mixed blessing near-death states are to a child's development. Even those who did not test out with extraordinarily high IQs evidenced uniquely creative minds, numerous faculty enhancements, unrelenting curiosity, and an exceptional ability to *know things* soon after reviving. Some were unusually gifted with foreign languages.

The majority of child experiencers are natural computer whizzes, not to mention top physicists and inventors, masters of the arts and humanities, and even professional psychics. Older teenage and adult experiencers are the ones who are most often drawn to healing, counseling, and ministerial roles afterward; this is not true of the majority of younger kids. Mention math or science and they're all aglow. And history intrigues them, as well as anything to do with times past.

Percentages show clearly a discrepancy between ability and interest and career choice: 93 percent are drawn to and highly proficient in math, science, and history, while only 25 percent are actually employed in those fields (40 percent if you consider the full 277 people involved in this study).

Why the glaring difference?

I offer the following case as an example of the kinds of challenges that can derail child experiencers. Bill from Atlanta, Georgia, "died" at about two months of age when an infant chair fell over on him, cutting off his airway. Early on he tried to tell his family about his near-death episode, but was slapped down harshly by his "wrath of God" southern Baptist grandmother and shunned, ignored, or teased by other members of his family, until he learned to keep quiet. He drove his first-grade teacher crazy remembering things randomly, like the time when she was helping the class read *See Spot Run* and he up and quoted from memory a long passage from *Robinson Crusoe*.

In my classical mechanics courses, I had what is best described as an intuitive grasp of everything I ever looked at. I would see a problem and immediately know the correct solution. Unfortunately, when I went to graduate school, where you have to explain how and why, I never finished my M.S. in physics. A professor in my graduate-level classical mechanics class once remarked, "If you say once more that it is 'intuitively obvious' concerning things that I and your classmates have to work out ten pages of complex equations to arrive at, I will give you not a C but an F in this class."

My analytical, mathematical, creative, and scientific skills have always been very good. I examine things and solve problems as if I had a parallel-processing system instead of a brain. This is very hard to explain, but it is almost as if most problems get broken down somewhere in my brain, the various portions of each are attacked by different subparts of my brain, and the solution is integrated and put together for me with no conscious effort

or control on my part. It is particularly frustrating for me
to deal with other people doing joint research or brain-
storming, because other people don't think like I do.
Please don't laugh—I get some of my best ideas from
dreams.

I am currently able to see all sides of an object at once.
I can read the "other" side of a box of Pop-Tarts without touching or moving the box. I have seen the insides
of locked objects at the same time that I saw all [their
outer] sides. It's not like they are unfolded and laid out
in two dimensions; it's more like looking at objects from
all possible angles *simultaneously*.

Bill has full-blown synesthesia (multiple sensing), is gifted
in many languages, and is self-taught in computers.

I once took a job at a company, and the job was operating a typesetting computer and interfacing and integrating it with the company's "main computer." There was
no manual for it and I received no training. In two days
I was making it do things the manufacturer said were
impossible.

Bill's brain as a child operated like a lightning calculator.
The only other person in his family who could do anything
similar was his mother, who had had a near-death experience as a teenager, but had never discussed it with anyone.
He felt that heredity was not a factor in explaining his or his
mother's mind—the phenomenon of near-death was.
Although Bill finally became a respectable physicist, he
didn't remain one, nor did he continue on with what could
have been a successful career in grand opera. Instead, he
became what he calls "a happy computer geek."

The bias against creative thought in the adult world, I submit, *is the reason why most people who experience near-death episodes as children seldom reach or maintain their full potential.*

And, according to my research, *85 percent of the kids with the greatest acceleration in mathematical ability also had a corresponding connection to music that was so passionate,* it felt like a love affair with the embrace of celestial harmonies. Many considered it better than sex. Curiously, those who showed no particular interest in or special response to music either lagged behind in math or didn't have the skill to begin with.

The parts of the brain that process math and music are located next to each other. Near-death states in children somehow seem to activate both of these areas together, *as if they were one unit.*

There is a link between spatial reasoning, mathematics, and music, in that all three are necessary to arrange schemes that encompass the many-sidedness or wholeness of a given design. As an example, music imparts harmony, how things resonate or fit together; mathematics supplies measurement, the specifics of physical manifestation. Yet it is spatial reasoning that, through creating an overall pattern, gives meaning and purpose to the task or item at hand, while ensuring that all parts fit the whole.

This ability to create an overall valid pattern is precisely where the kids shine, for *the average child experiencer becomes a spatial/nonverbal/sensory-dynamic thinker afterward*—regardless of gender.

I was able to show in *Beyond the Light* how varying degrees of physiological aftereffects (especially as regard light, sound, and electrical sensitivity) are related to the intensity of exposure to light during the near-death episode. It was the *intensity of light,* not the length of exposure, that determined these effects.

Among children I discovered some fascinating contradictions to my previous work, and they center around the issue of genius.

Near-death experiences, *if sufficiently intense,* seem to trigger faster and more complex growth spurts in children's brains than would be expected for children of their age. The more intense the experience the bigger the growth spurt, including relative intelligence increases sometimes to the point of genius.

In the previous chapter, I reported finding clusters of children's near-death states at certain ages. Birth to fifteen months and three to five years are the age groupings during which most of the events occurred. *These two clusters accounted for 81 percent of the genius-level intelligence I found in my research,* indicating to me that the younger the child the more susceptible he or she is to the sudden charge of intensity from a near-death episode. (Brain circuitry formation normally skyrockets in infancy; three- to five-year-olds undergo temporal lobe development as they experience the birth of imagination and creative thought.)

The Darkness That Knows is a major component of scenarios for the youngest of experiencers. This unique, warm, friendly, living, loving, pulsating, all-knowing darkness is described by little ones (as soon as they are verbal) in terms evocative of a passionate embrace. Their body language, facial expressions, often a shaking or quivering voice that they use when trying to find words to portray this darkness, are unmistakable. This darkness is not frightening, nor is it a state of suspension or void or lifeless nothingness. This darkness has a brilliance all its own and an enfolding shimmer that is, for them, love's fullness.

Significantly, I found more compelling cases of genius *specifically associated with infants and toddlers who experienced the*

Darkness That Knows, than with their counterparts who were bathed in light.

Because of this, I am moved to ask, What if children can have temporal lobe *enhancement* before they are old enough to experience temporal lobe *development?* Would that account for the phenomenal abstractions a child displays after a near-death experience? What if the learning reversals so apparent in child experiencers are the direct result of the brain being "charged" by the intensity of either an unusual light effect or dark effect at crucial junctures in its growth? What if there is more involved in the outworking of a near-death scenario than can be explained by the study of either the human brain or the human family?

What if the near-death experience in children is a second birth, a repositioning of brain/mind structures from regular genetic patterning to more expansive capacities and an acceleration of intellect that makes the children part of the groundwork evolution lays for the next "upgrade" in our species?

Let me go further with this.

There are three styles of learning and at least seven distinct types of intelligence. The three learning styles are visual, auditory, and tactile-kinesthetic. Most people are familiar with these but unfamiliar with the fact that intelligence can manifest in so many different ways. Psychologist Howard Gardner, famous for his insights into genius, posits that society's concept of intelligence is far too limiting. In his book *Frames of Mind*[4] he argues that Western society as a whole and schools in particular force linguistics and logic/mathematics on kids while neglecting other ways of knowing. He identifies the seven types of intelligence as linguistic, logical-mathematical, spatial, bodily-kinesthetic, musical, interpersonal (more social, outwardly directed), and intrapersonal (self-paced, inwardly directed).

It is important that we accept this broader concept of intelligence to appreciate that the genius I observed in child experiencers was not confined to linguistics or logic or even what we normally think of when we refer to visual and/or auditory and tactile learners. *What I saw was what I call "true genius," where intuition is the equal of intellect; where the brain seemed to evidence parallel-processing systems, faculty enhancements, multiple sensing, the simultaneous presence of multiple brain-wave patterns, and an ability to know things unbounded by the constraints of past, present, and future, as if they could access and draw from a cosmic bank of knowledge.*

True genius is the goal of transcendental meditation, various types of spiritual and religious practices, and enlightenment; it is the idea of reaching oneness with Source. Few probationers on the spiritual path ever reach this goal, and fewer still are able to maintain the state once they reach it.

It would be an exaggeration for me to claim that children who have near-death experiences are able to maintain such a high state of brain-mind functioning, but many of them do reach this state and evidence that they did with typical aftereffects.

How many actually develop and refine what they achieved by virtue of their second birth?

Precious few.

Too much too soon may be the reason why, along with the stress of readjusting to the social groups they must somehow fit back into. The conundrum: How can educators be expected to teach a child who knows more than they do? Yet how can a child be expected to attend to a teacher who is utterly boring and has absolutely nothing of interest to offer?

Hence, most child experiencers go through some period of rejection afterward, both of home and of school, that leads them either to act out feelings of anger, rage, and resentment or to withdraw due to feelings of loss, abandonment, and depression. Fortunately, many are able to turn the situation around, if not in the lower grades, then by high school or in college. I find it fascinating that a third of those who filled out the questionnaire had another near-death episode in adulthood that they said healed the confusion of their earlier one. This underscores another force at work—a spiritual dimension.

Theresa Csanady of Glenview, Illinois, suggested that I investigate the field of gifted children in my search for links to the spiritual dimension of intelligence. What I found has a direct bearing on the uniqueness of near-death kids, for those qualities that identify a gifted child are *virtually the same* as those that describe child experiencers.

Linda Kreger Silverman, Ph.D., a psychologist and director of the Gifted Child Development Center in Denver, Colorado, is a leader in this field, and she has given me permission to list the characteristics of gifted children that she has identified in her research:[5]

- Gifted children often have unique learning styles; they learn in different ways from other children.
- They also learn at a faster pace. They solve problems rapidly.
- They are usually developmentally advanced. They learn to talk, walk, read, etc., earlier than usual.
- They may appear healthier, physically stronger, and better coordinated than their agemates.
- They are very curious and tend to ask complex questions.
- They also give complicated answers. Their detailed explanations show that they have greater depth of understanding of topics than their classmates.

- They are quick to recognize relationships, even relationships that others do not see.
- They organize information in new ways, creating new perspectives.
- They often see many solutions to a problem.
- Their thinking is more abstract than their classmates', involving hypothetical possibilities rather than present realities.
- They often see ambiguity in what appears to be factual information.
- *They have large vocabularies and tend to express themselves well.*
- They have unusually good memories.
- *They may be natural leaders. They may initiate and organize activities for others.*
- They also enjoy working independently. They easily become absorbed in the mastery of skills.
- *They may prefer the company of older children and adults.*
- *They may like to be best at everything, and may refuse to participate in activities in which they might fail.*★
- *They are often perfectionists, becoming very upset if things don't turn out as they expect. Sometimes they compare themselves and their achievements to great persons they have read about rather than to others their own age.*★
- *They are not necessarily gifted in all areas.*
- They usually don't want their giftedness pointed out.

Italics are my own and indicate areas of deviation. Regarding large vocabularies, natural leadership, a preference for the company of older people, and limitations in gifts, these traits were true with some child experiencers, but not true overall. The starred items signify a definite *no*. I say this because I have seen only a few kids out of all of those I have interviewed who were competitive or perfectionists by Silverman's standard. These two missing traits are significant.

The average near-death survivor, child or adult, couldn't care less if goals are fulfilled, deadlines met, or awards won. What motivates them is quite different. Silverman included in the material she provided me a monograph about Dabrowski's theory of emotional development.[6] Kazimierz Dabrowski, a Polish psychologist and psychiatrist, based his theory of emotional development on the study of sensitive, nonaggressive, highly intelligent, and creative individuals. Through neurological examination, he documented that creatively gifted individuals had more pronounced responses to various types of stimuli. He called this "overexcitability" and equated it to an abundance of physical energy, heightened acuity of the senses, vivid imagination, intellectual curiosity and drive, and a deep capacity to care. *The greater the strength of these traits, the greater the potential for an ethical, compassionate path in adulthood.*

His discovery dovetails with what I have consistently seen in child experiencers.

Truly, youngsters who have undergone a near-death episode stand out. I call them the "second-born" because of the following telltale characteristics:

Elements of a Second Birth
- Those hardly born can undergo a second birth.
- Temporal lobe expansion can precede or accelerate natural development.
- The learning curve can reverse itself, placing abstract conceptualizing before foundational understanding.
- IQ enhancements and faculty extensions can accompany heightened spatial/nonverbal/sensory-dynamic thinking, giving rise to creative problem-solving skills.

- An awareness of future can clarify the earth world of time and space, by engendering "rehearsals" that provide for advance preparation in meeting life demands.
- Sensing multiples can open up whole new worlds of possibility and new dimensions of what is real.
- Brain shifts can jump-start the engine of evolution, enabling the human species to adapt to ever-changing needs and pressures.
- Spirit shifts can advance attitudes and behaviors toward social justice and moral integrity, as compassion and caring replace the obsessions that drive greed.
- The higher mind can emerge as the higher brain develops, thanks to structural and chemical changes that occur in the brain after a brain shift and in the heart because of its realignment after a spirit shift.

It is my belief that the formula evolution uses to guarantee renewal and rebirth in the human family, and the continuous cycling of *the Second Coming* (that transcendent enlightenment that lifts us to the next octave of existence), is brain shift/spirit shift—the engine that drives evolution . . . the mechanism that enables us to make quantum leaps in our development as a species.

FOUR

JUMBLES OF GOOD AND EVIL

All have their own personal ways of acting according to their visions. We must learn to be different, to feel and taste the manifold things that are us.

Lame Deer

The grandiosity of theorizing about a child experiencer's possible second birth is unconscionable if we ignore the reality behind the theory—the positive and negative aspects of how kids really respond to transformational events; *what they think.* By taking a few moments to see through their eyes, we can begin to appreciate the fuller scope of our subject. This will prepare us for an in-depth look at the impact of aftereffects, covered in the next chapter.

Here is a brief sampling of comments that should dispel any notion that a baby's mind is a blank slate:

As a baby I was very observant. I "knew" certain things. I understood what death was and could tell when each of my two grandparents who lived with us in the same building were going to die.
Margaret Evans, Roscoe, Illinois.
NDE-like experience at age seven, dramatic death dream

The tiny person perched at the head of my crib said, "You're a baby." I remember glancing up at a nearby mirror and catching my reflection, that of a baby lying in a crib, then of grabbing a foot and sticking it in my mouth and biting down. "Yup, this is me," I replied. "This is real. I really am a baby. Wow, isn't this something!"
Dorothy M. Bernstein, North Olmsted, Ohio.
NDE at ages ten months and three and a
half years, both suffocation

Some children's memories begin *before* birth, as in the case of Carroll Gray of Atlanta, Georgia: "Red, warm, wet fear. Voices raised in anger somewhere nearby. Not a childlike perspective, but an adult awareness of what anger is. Voices were male and female. A sense of alarm. Something drastically not as it should be. Male accusing female of killing his son."

Two weeks previously, the doctor had informed Gray's mother that there was no heartbeat, that the baby was dead. At the moment of this particular memory, Carroll's father, screaming and enraged, grabbed his wife and sent her flying across the room, right into the corner of a large table, causing her amniotic sac to rupture. The mother was rushed to the hospital, where a "dead" baby girl was delivered via an emergency cesarean section. To everyone's astonishment, the child began to breathe.

The case of Carroll Gray typifies something that I've found to be commonplace among children's near-death experiences, and that is the jumbling together of good and evil. For kids, the prospect of "wearing" a body, even the act of breathing, lacks definable edges. What we regard as a blessing may be horrific to them, or vice versa.

Carroll went on to have numerous near-death scenarios, starting twenty-four hours after her emergency delivery.

The fragmented speech pattern she uses is how she remembers thinking at the time. "Looking down at the baby from above, through the glass of the thing it's in [the incubator]. It's tiny. Unfinished. Its head open from forehead to base of skull. Brain under something like gelatin. Skin yellow. Fingers and toes blackened. Purple blotches. Body fur, more like an animal than a human. Tubes, needles. On its back. It can't breathe—no one has noticed that it can't breathe. It's me. I recognize the hands and feet as mine. But this is wrong. Anxiety. Alarm. I'm not supposed to be here. A mistake. Fear. Sorrow for the baby. Born too soon and already traumatized by the loud anger it absorbed in the red stuff. That kept it small, too. Head the size of soap ball, eleven inches long. Two pounds and dropping. It's not going to make it. I can't fit into something that small, and I'm not supposed to. Sense of being in the wrong place. Supposed to be somewhere else. Late for . . . something." The attending physician warned Carroll's parents that the baby could not possibly survive, and thus obtained permission from them to try thirty-one experimental procedures on the infant.

Carroll remembers looking at "the baby" in the glass thing three days later and determining that its heart and lungs were working but its stomach wasn't. "Little lashes. Eyes moving under thin lids. Not my face. After all, it's a baby and I'm not. It might just make it. Is that good or bad?" The attending physician reported bad nights followed by rallies, though nothing hopeful. Yet against all odds, the child lived.

Eight months had passed when Carroll Gray's father took a sharp pencil and drove it through her stomach. It entered below the right rib cage and exited to the right of her spine. She floated free of her body. "The living room is in disarray, a heavy platform rocker and two lamps knocked over. The man, disheveled and apparently intoxicated and angry, leaning over the baby, screaming for it to stop crying. The baby lies on an end table, impaled on the pencil, gasping jerky breaths, gushing blood, its right little finger facing toward its shoulder. No feeling of pain, or connection to the baby at all. Realization that the pencil has missed major vital organs but that it may die anyway. No wish to return to its tiny body." The pediatrician, a drinking buddy of the father, never reported the abuse to the authorities.

On a snowy winter day two years later, Carroll's father strapped her by the waist to a sled and set out on a brisk hike to the home of a friend. He went inside to visit. Hours later he remembered that he'd left his daughter outside. By then, she had contracted pneumonia and was in the first stages of hypothermia. Her near-death scenario this time was lengthy and focused on a walk she took along a curving wall of white light to the right of a mist. A grown-up soon accompanied her. He was tall and slender, with a kind face and thinning hair. He wore a shirt, pants with suspenders, practical shoes, and a vest with something shiny on it—a watch chain that glinted light. He allowed her to pick his pocket and pull on the chain. A gold watch slid out. "For a moment I am me and the toddler at the same time. The toddler cannot read, but I can. The watch is not running; it stopped at 1:17. I smile. He smiles. I put it back and pull on the other side of the chain. On it is a small gold shiny thing. It has curlicues on it. The curlicues on one side are writing in English, the toddler's first name, on what I recognize as a small, two-bladed pocketknife. On the other side, a little shield surrounded by a flower garland with the year 1917 on it. I look up at him. 'That's my name.' He smiles, nods. 'It's all right, I'm the other Carroll.' He smiles again. 'It's yours. Remember.' I nod. The shiny thing is mine. Neat. I'll remember." The man let her choose the direction in which she might continue to walk. She looked both ways, shrugged, then returned the way she had come, into a dark, peaceful, unscary tunnel.

At the age of two and a half, in front of both parents, Carroll Gray repeated back to her father *every word he had said when he threw his pregnant wife into the table. She also described the situation and furniture placement.* Her parents were dumbfounded. No one knew the full story of what had occurred, nor had they discussed it between themselves. A short time later, she detailed *what she had once looked like and how she had been cared for "in the glass thing," her impalement with the pencil, and her ordeal on the sled.*

Afterward, she told her grandmother about the man who had walked next to her along the white wall. Her grandmother, suspicious of who it might be, opened the family album to a page with numerous pictures of many people. *Carroll immediately identified the grandfather who had died two years before her birth,* and for whom she had been named. She then related with great accuracy every facet of his watch, chain, and gold pocketknife, including the time the watch had stopped and the date on the pocketknife, but was unable to convince anyone that the grandfather had given those treasures to her. They remained tucked away in a glass case until, twenty years later, her mother, while sorting through papers, happened upon the grandfather's will. In reading it, she was flabbergasted to learn that he had bequeathed his watch, chain, and gold pocketknife to his granddaughter and namesake. At the time of his death he had no granddaughter or namesake, nor did anyone have any inkling that he expected to have one, or that through perhaps an act of precognition he was privy to futuristic knowledge. Carroll finally got the treasures her grandfather had promised her when she "died" at the age of two.

At twelve, Carroll survived death yet again when she had a severe attack of asthma. She then "died" five more times in adulthood from varied health crises, each time experiencing another near-death scenario, making a total of ten, in addition to the prebirth incident. Her father, resentful that she lived, continued his villainy until she was forced to seek legal protection. "The monster died last year," she confided to me. "At last, I'm free."

Throughout Carroll Gray's story, regardless of her age at the time, we can recognize the workings of a decidedly mature mind that is stunningly accurate in what it perceives. This oddity was displayed by *every child experiencer* I ever interviewed, *irrespective of age*. It's as if consciousness can function quite apart from personality, and, in so doing, is aware of other agendas—perhaps the mission of the soul. Carroll's case, though, implies that the traditional understanding of soul plans as being divinely guided may not always be true.

Children do not process their near-death states as do adults, nor do they regard them in the same fashion. A case in point: "I was very small when I had my near-death experience. When I could run and play like the other kids again, I'd go from room to room. I'd look under the beds, in the closets, behind the doors and furniture—from the top of the house to the bottom—other people's houses, too. I'd look and look but I never found them [the beings of light who had visited her]. They loved me. I know they did. They were warm and wonderful and bright with light. They came to me when I died and they left when I breathed again. I looked for years and years. Sometimes I'd curl up underneath my bed and cry. Why couldn't I find them? Where did they go? Why did they leave me in a place where no one cared and no one loved me? Was I that bad that they couldn't return?"

The teenager who spoke these words was four years old when her heart stopped and beings made of light came to get her. She recalls walking hand in hand with them into realms of music and joy and beauty, and so much love that she wanted never to leave. Then, suddenly, without choice or warning, she revived and found herself back in a body racked with pain. Surrounded by strangers, she was forced to deal, alone and frightened, with the aftermath of major surgery. She has yet to recover from the shock and the anger at feeling abandoned, *not by her parents or the medical staff,* interestingly enough, *but by the "bright ones" who loved her and then left her behind.* She now sees a counselor and has requested anonymity.

Stories of children's near-death scenarios are compellingly heavenlike, innocent renderings of the pure lands our hearts *know* must somehow exist on the other side of death's door. The cases of little ones, we say, confirm that life is everlasting. Yet the foregoing experiencers I have quoted are examples of what I keep hearing from the young, especially those who "died" as preteens and can compare "before" with "after."

Clearly, children can be and often are more confused and disoriented by their near-death episodes than by any life-threatening event that precipitated it. Listen to these voices:

Laura, San Francisco, California. NDE at age three and a half, child abuse. "For many years, I simply wanted to die again and go back."

Emily, Seattle, Washington. NDE at age two, high fever; at five from complications during surgery. "I wanted to go back in my dreams. I looked for The Light in the hall closet downstairs. I felt loved there. I was saddened when I could not find The Light. I missed The People. I liked them very much."

Regina Patrick, Toledo, Ohio. NDE at age four, pneumonia. "Afterward, I was concerned that 'they' would be mad at me for forgetting the instructions they gave me."

Janet Blessing, Pittsfield, Massachusetts. NDE at age nine months, pneumonia. "I felt so homesick afterward. I regretted being in the flesh again, cut off from the Voice of God/Source of Guidance. I oscillated between periods of great elation and creativity and deep suicidal depression as a teenager."

Mary Cosgrove, San Francisco, California. NDE at age thirteen, severe meningitis. "I recall not really wanting to 'wake up' or 'get well.' My initial reaction was confusion, guilt, even some anger during my recovery. I told no one about it. I was in a quandary of sorts, feeling different, as though I was from another place or family. I wanted to return, and finally tried to by slashing my wrists at twenty."

P. Ann Baillie, Ann Arbor, Michigan. NDE at age three months, hypothermia; at five months from drowning. "Being sent back into this mess of a family has often felt like a betrayal. Being loved and welcomed briefly on the other side and then returned into a loveless world was sometimes more than I could bear, especially because I could not seem to kill myself and I wanted to."

Lois Bradford, South Dakota. NDE at age four, complications during surgery. "Psychologists were telling me my problem was a projection from my parents, yet I had come to terms with my inadequate human parents. As horrendous as my history of sexual abuse is, and the ongoing abuse by my family members, *nothing* is as traumatic as the spiritual implications of being rejected by God. You can't believe the horror of this. I was bad and God confirmed it."

Tom Meeres, southern New Jersey. NDE-like experience at age fourteen, severe reaction to death dream. "I was so disassociated from ordinary perception afterward that I couldn't even imagine how to live the rest of my life. Something as ordinary as getting out of bed and leaving the relative safety of the bedroom seemed frightening. I had no idea how to relate to other people anymore, leading to long periods of depression during the next twenty-odd years."

All of these experiencers had positive, uplifting scenarios. All of them! They found their true "home" and wanted to stay there, but couldn't.

The result?

One-third of those in my study of childhood near-death states turned to alcohol for solace within five to ten years of their near-death experiences (the incidence rate with adult experiencers is about one in five). Over half dealt with serious bouts of depression afterward (adults have a slightly higher incidence). Twenty-one percent actually attempted suicide (this is an exceptionally high rate, compared to less than 4 percent of adult experiencers). None who sought to re-create their episode through the use of drugs was successful (the same is true of adult experiencers).

Among adults, the near-death experience is, for the most part, a suicide deterrent. Unfortunately, the same cannot be said of children.

Numerous experiencers have admitted to me that they became alcoholics as children *because they couldn't handle the aftermath of coming back from where they had been.* Those who tried to kill themselves *did so as a way to return "home."* Kids who had their episodes while they were of school age were much more likely to be affected by such extremes than those who "died" in infancy or as a toddler. Among the

experiencers I interviewed, *how the episode ended,* especially
if abrupt, proved to be the deciding factor in their response.

We need to realize that children tend to personalize whatever happens to them. Hence, if they are left with a sense of:

Loss	It's their fault "everyone went away," and they feel guilty.
Rejection	They're bad, and they feel ashamed.
Betrayal	They're unworthy, and they feel abandoned.
Acceptance	It's okay to leave "home," and they feel satisfied.
Joy	They're trustworthy, and they feel confident.
Love	They are extra special, and they feel secure.

Child experiencers tend to repress their feelings until
some unexpected incident (usually in adulthood) triggers
what lies tucked away within their deepest self. Delayed
aftereffects are commonplace. Regardless of the challenges
adult experiencers face, kids have it tougher. Adults can at
least speak up for themselves or exercise a fair degree of
choice. Should a child say anything about an experience, he
or she is usually ignored or hushed. Although many youngsters are able to integrate their near-death experiences successfully, the reverse is also true.

Good and evil can indeed jumble together in children's
cases, as is further evidenced by the next two cases. Nathan
Kyles III of El Campo, Texas, was almost eleven when, with
his brother Dale, he was given permission to splash around
in a motel swimming pool while an older cousin applied
for work.

"I got out of the water and walked inside to where my
cousin was. When we were ready to leave, my cousin asked
me, 'Where is Dale?' The first thing that came to my mind

was the pool. I ran back to the deep end and saw my brother looking up at me from the bottom. I bent over and somehow grabbed his hand, but he pulled me in. Now I am on the bottom with my eyes closed, scared, trying to call my cousin, thinking I am about to die. Every time I opened my mouth I swallowed more water. Then I felt my life leave me. To this day, before God, I swear that everything good or bad that I had ever done passed right before my eyes. I felt a hand grab my shirt collar and snatch me out of the pool, but nobody was there. When I opened my eyes, I saw that my brother was already out. My cousin didn't know how to swim, so he didn't save us. Years later, we were talking about it, and the other two told me a white woman saved us. Nobody knew her. After she pulled us out, they said, she just disappeared."

Nathan's next comment echoes what is said by many child experiencers: "Afterward, I blocked all of this from my mind."

In Nathan's case, once he returned home after his close call with death, his mother told him to shut up before he could offer a single word, then she whipped both boys for leaving the house. His later attempts at communication were also rebuked. Guilt and shame came to overlay the miracle of his experience, not because of his episode, per se, but because of the way his family treated him after he came home. Certainly his mother was worried about her children and, to that degree, her reaction was understandable. Still, the question remains: Would Nathan have turned out differently if she had let him speak? After the whipping, *Nathan didn't care anymore.* His grades immediately plummeted. His teacher became alarmed and called on his mother, but she couldn't get him to listen, either. Within the span of one year, he turned from a positive, studious, happy, thoughtful child to a sullen criminal who didn't give a damn about anything or anyone.

Nathan explained: "Before it happened, I was never in trouble with the law. After it happened, I started stealing, burglarizing houses and buildings. My whole way of thinking changed. I was about twelve when I went to jail for the first time. I got caught stealing some old coins out of a lady's purse while playing with her son. The judge kicked me out of town for a year, and I had to live with my father nine hundred miles away. When I returned, I went downhill further." A long litany of difficulties followed, beginning with a prison term at the age of nineteen for parole violation. Charges of burglary, terrorist threats, and harassment were later dropped because it was proved he had not committed them. When he was released, however, he promptly stole again and wound up back in prison. "I stayed in prison this time for nine years and two months. I was sent to a halfway house because my mom had died earlier and my parole plan was all messed up. I started smoking marijuana, I guess for comfort at my mom being dead. So, while in the halfway house, I was written up for violating their rules, which was also a violation of my parole. Again, my parole was revoked, and here I sit in prison for the fourth time."

It would take some digging to determine if Nathan, an African American, was a victim of racial prejudice, as his punishment seems outlandish considering the crimes he committed. But it wouldn't take any digging at all to pinpoint the moment he underwent a personality change that radically altered his life for the worse.

Nathan's case opens the door to the topic of family reactions and how deceptively complicated they can become. The following account, although filled with miracles, dramatically illustrates the extremes kids can face when family members feel threatened by the near-death phenomenon.

Lynn from Michigan underwent open-heart surgery at

thirteen to correct a condition she had had almost since birth. She was unable to run and play with the other kids, and she would on occasion turn blue and get sick. A large black Great Dane named Harvey was her constant companion and best buddy. "The last thing I remember in surgery was a male voice saying in a very matter-of-fact way, 'Uh-oh, we have a problem here.' The next thing I knew I was floating around the ceiling looking down on my body. My chest was open wide and I could see my internal organs. I remember thinking how odd it was that my organs were a beautiful pearl gray, not at all like the bright red chunks in the horror flicks I loved to watch. I also noticed there was a black doctor and an Oriental one on the operating team. The reason this stuck in my mind is that I was brought up in a very white middle-class neighborhood, and I had seen black schoolteachers but never a black doctor. I'd met the operating team the day before, but they were all white.

"Suddenly, I had to move on, so I floated into the waiting room, where my parents were. My father had his head buried in my mother's lap. He was kneeling at her feet, his arms wrapped around her waist, and he was sobbing. My mother was stroking his head, whispering to him. This scene shocked me, as my father was not prone to showing emotions. Once I realized they would be fine, I felt myself pulled into a horizontal tunnel.

"The ride through the tunnel was like nothing else. I remember thinking, 'So this is death.' The tunnel was dark, and every once in a while something that looked like lightning would flash across my path. These flashes were brilliant in color and didn't scare me. At the end of the tunnel was a bright light.

"From the light came two dogs of mine. One was a collie named Mimi who had died three years previously from an infection, and the other was a boxer named Sam who had died two years before after being hit by a car. The dogs came running and jumped on me and kissed my face with their tongues. Their tongues weren't wet, and I felt no weight when they jumped on me. The dogs seemed to glow from a light that was inside them. I recall saying to myself, 'Thank you, God, for letting my dogs be alive.' I hugged my dogs as tight as I could.

"I then called my dogs and together we started walking toward the light. All colors were in the light and it was warm, a living thing, and there were people as far as the eye could see, and they were glowing with an inner light—just like my dogs. In the distance I could see fields, hills, and a sky. The light spoke and it said, 'Lynn, it is not time for you yet. Go back, child.' I put my hand up to touch the top of the light. I knew then that I had touched the face of God. I told God that I loved Him, and I wanted to stay with Him. Again the light said, 'Lynn, go back. It is not time for you. You have work to do for me. Go back.'

"I know this sounds silly, but I asked the light, 'If I go, can I come back and will my dogs still be here waiting for me?' The light said yes, and then told me there were people who wanted to see me before I left. From out of the light came my maternal grandparents. I ran to them and embraced them. They were going to walk me part of the way back. Just as I was turning to leave, a man stepped from the light. He wore a full dress uniform, U.S. Navy. He was very tall and very blond, with blue eyes. I had never seen the man before, but he knew me and smiled.

" 'I am your uncle Franklin. Tell Dorothy that I'm okay and that the baby is with me. Tell her I never stopped loving her and that I am glad she got on with her life. Tell her that when her time comes, I will come for her. Remember to tell her I love her.' As I turned, the man shouted, 'Tell Dorothy, tell her you met Franklin and I'm okay and so is the baby.'

"My grandparents told me if I stayed any longer I might not make it back. But I wanted to talk with Jesus. I had a very important question to ask him. A beam of light, different from yet similar to the first one, covered me. I knew this light was Christ. I leaned against it for one moment and then asked my question. 'Dear Jesus, is it true that you gave me this heart condition so that I would have a cross to carry like you did?' (Sister Agnes, my sixth-grade teacher, had told me that my heart condition was my cross to bear for Christ.) I heard the voice of Christ vibrate through me as he said, 'No, this heart condition of yours is not a cross from me for you to bear. This heart condition is a challenge to help you grow and stay compassionate. Now, go back.'

"As I walked back, my grandmother told me that my father was going to leave my mother and that I would be my mother's strength. I saw people hiding in the tunnel, people who were afraid to come into the light or who were disoriented about where they were. I expressed concern for them but was told not to worry, as a guide would be along to help them. Some of these people looked like soldiers. Then I remembered Vietnam and I knew where the soldiers were coming from."

Lynn detailed what it was like to be resuscitated and then wake up hours later hooked up to a myriad of tubes. She recalls being unable to speak and being fascinated by shadows moving among the medical staff, shadows she came to realize were people who had died there. She claims it didn't take long before she could watch death take place—to see the soul as it exited the body. Her doctor released her after a month because he was afraid that all the time she spent talking to dead or misplaced souls would drive her crazy. Her early release pleased her father, as if it gave him an excuse to be cold and unemotional again.

"The day I left, in front of my parents, I asked Dr. Davidson who the black doctor was in the operating room. Dr. Davidson said he had been called in at the last minute when one of the team members became ill. He wanted to know if this doctor had been by to say hi, but I said no, I saw him during surgery. Dr. Davidson stopped smiling and told me to go home and forget everything."

Once Lynn returned home, her life changed. Lightbulbs would pop if she got angry, and formerly inanimate objects would move around of their own accord (the research term for this is psychokinesis). She would see images whenever she touched anything (synesthesia). From touching jewelry, she could tell who owned it and where it had been worn (psychometry). When she looked at a person, she could see their life in flashes, including their future (clairvoyance). School became easy, as she no longer had to study to get really good grades (intelligence enhancement). But sunshine bothered her, and so did loud noise.

"My father left us. In front of the whole family, he told me he thought I was crazy and belonged in a mental hospital. It was Thanksgiving Day, one year after my surgery. I told my father I could prove I wasn't crazy. I turned to Aunt Dorothy and said, 'Who is Franklin?' There was silence. Every eye at the table was on me; mouths were wide open. My uncle George, who was married to my aunt Dorothy, looked at me with tears in his eyes and said, 'Lynn, if you wanted to hurt me, you've done a good job.'

"Everyone went home early and my father left us. A few weeks later my aunt wanted to know how I knew about Franklin. I told her exactly what had happened during surgery. Then my aunt led me up to her attic and unlocked a large trunk. (I had never been in her attic before, nor had I seen the trunk.) She pulled out pictures of the man I had seen in the light. My aunt told me that she had married Franklin during World War II, after a brief twenty-four-hour courtship. She had been engaged to Uncle George at the time, but left him for Franklin. My aunt started to cry as she told me that she and Franklin were very happy together for two months, and then he was shipped out. After he left, she discovered she was pregnant. When she was seven months along, my aunt received word that my uncle had been killed in the invasion of Italy. He was on the lead ship dropping off troops. The news caused her to miscarry. She hemorrhaged so badly that a complete hysterectomy had to be performed to save her. The next year Uncle George married her and destroyed all pictures of Franklin, requesting that everyone in the family never speak Franklin's name again. The only pictures to survive were those Aunt Dorothy hid in the trunk."

With this final verification of what she had seen during her near-death experience, Lynn became openly confident and trusting, although she preferred solitude to a social life. She lost all fear of death, changed her diet to include less meat, began to exhibit steadily increasing displays of psychic abilities, and became a friend of ghosts.

Yet the guilt she felt about her father's actions and what he did to her Great Dane still haunts her. "He took my dog when he left, and he'd call me on the phone and accuse me of being possessed by the devil, saying I had to become a Christian or he'd kill my dog. And while we'd be talking he'd beat my dog so I could hear him cry out in pain. He did this with phone call after phone call until he killed my dog with me on the line listening. I couldn't believe my father actually did it until that night, when Harvey's soul came to say good-bye and let me know he was okay. For years afterward I'd have coughing fits where I could hardly breathe. It wasn't until I reached adulthood that I connected the coughing to my pent-up emotions about my dog's death."

After years of counseling, Lynn has yet to release the grief she feels about her near-death experience. "My father walked out on our family because of me, because of how I changed after my episode, and my relationship with my uncle was never the same again. My family was badly hurt and my dog was killed, and it's all my fault."

Lynn's case speaks volumes about the phenomenon called near-death, and how it can be both a blessing and a nightmare. What she went through shows us that integrating the experience is *a very sensitive issue for the young,* one that has never before been adequately addressed.

FIVE

THE IMPACT OF AFTEREFFECTS

Deep in their roots all flowers keep the light.

Theodore Roethke

It takes a child experiencer to understand a child experiencer.

A young man, preferring to call himself A Child from Minnesota, was suffocated at the age of three and a half by an older brother. He has this to say about the challenge of experiencing the near-death phenomenon as a youngster:

Children react differently to near-death episodes than adults because the set of experiences they have to compare them with is smaller. To an adult, such a phenomenon is only one of many life occurrences. But to a child, a near-death experience is the world itself, or "all there is." A child has a more difficult time "drawing the line" between what is eternal and what is earthly. Children are forced to rely on the experience more, simply because they lack what adults can draw from. This colors everything children think, say, and do.

Speaking for myself, I have come to understand that the long-term effects of this phenomenon have been very large indeed. These effects include (1) an ability to desensitize the self from physical sensations; (2) an ability to communicate through nonverbal and nonauditory means; (3) a partial loss of ability to communicate verbally and auditorily; (4) problems reintegrating the ethereal self back into the physical self; and (5) challenges interacting socially.

My experience of being out of body enabled me to learn very young how to perform the separation of body and spirit. My understanding of the process, however, was unconscious. I did not know what I was doing or how I was doing it until much later. This first experience arose as a result of intense pain, so, in the beginning, I used this skill simply to avoid pain. Since the skill itself was unconscious, it quickly became a knee-jerk reaction to discomfort of all sorts. Eventually, I came to remain in that state as much as possible. This led to an inability to function socially. As I desensitized myself to my own feelings, I was equally unable to feel the pain or joy of others. And, as I explored this state, emotions, people, and all of social life grew ever more foreign to me—I grew ever more withdrawn. I have come to believe that body and spirit need to nourish each other, and cannot remain separate indefinitely.

Almost every child experiencer becomes adept at dissociation, as did A Child from Minnesota. The term "dissociation" was formerly used in the field of psychiatry as a label to describe an individual who withdrew or severed any association with his or her body and/or environment. It was considered an aberrant, unhealthy mental state. Current thinking on the subject has shifted considerably as more mental health professionals are now recognizing that dissociation may actually be a natural by-product of consciousness as it develops along new lines of thought and creative imagination,[1] that it is more a sign of adaptation than insanity. But, as A Child from Minnesota finally learned, even positive skills that enrich our lives can become crutches.

Without a supportive framework of understanding in the wake of a near-death episode, a child experiencer can easily feel as if he or she is either stupid, crazy, or suddenly "foreign." Family and friends who are unaware of what such an experience can entail may find the child's sudden behavior changes either frightening or perhaps an attention-getting ploy, maybe even the product of an overactive imagination.

The full profile of physiological and psychological aftereffects appeared early in chapter 2. What follows are more questionnaire results to give us a deeper look at how these aftereffects impact a child's life.

Significant increase in allergies	45%
Became vegetarian	18%
Unusual sensitivity to light	
decreased tolerance	59%
increased tolerance	20%
Unusual sensitivity to sound	
decreased tolerance	74%
enhanced desire for classical music	41%
Electrical sensitivity	52%
Health	
still dealing with handicaps from death event	32%
went on to have major illnesses in adulthood	30%
blood pressure substantially lower after episode	27%
feel as if bodymind was rewired/reconfigured	41%
direct improvement in health after episode	45%
state of health now—excellent	77%
—challenged	23%

Psychic enhancements

more intuitive	64%
more precognitive	73%
more knowing	48%
more of an active, vivid dream life	66%
conscious future memory episodes	34%
visible manifestations of spirit	27%

Unusual connection to nature/animals   66%

Spiritual inclination

mystical	66%
religious	25%

Relationship with parents/siblings after

better	30%
alienated	57%

Relationship with friends/strangers after

open/friendly	27%
became a loner	57%

Marriage

once, long-lasting	41%
twice, second one long-lasting	16%
divorced, never remarried	23%
single, never married	20%

Attitude toward money

careful and responsible	30%
disinterested, doesn't "give a hoot"	66%

Attitude toward job

loves to work	80%
doesn't like to work (or unemployable)	16%

Homeowner   68%

Mission

knows exactly what it is and is doing it	45%
has a sense of what it might be but no details	32%
doesn't have a clue	23%

Immediate response to episode afterward

positive	34%
negative	61%

Desires to return to the Other Side

yes	41%
no	43%
learned how to return at will	9%

Regrets about the near-death experience

yes	32%
no	57%

Aftereffects

decreased with time	9%
increased with time	73%
remained the same	18%

Note: Concerning counseling, only 27% ever obtained any. Of that number, only 52% were helped to any degree.

COMPARISON WITH ADULT EXPERIENCERS

If we compare research results between child experiencers and adults (as detailed in *Beyond the Light*), we will see some startling differences. To begin with, 57 percent of child experiencers went on to enjoy long-lasting marriages once grown (whether married once or twice). Adult experiencers, on the other hand, report having tremendous difficulty afterward forming or maintaining stable relationships; 78 percent of their marriages end in divorce.

Both groups experience unusual increases or decreases in light sensitivity: about 79 percent of the kids (this includes both tolerance-level changes), which is close to the adult range of 80 to 90 percent. Whereas 73 percent of adults evidence electrical sensitivity, only 52 percent of the kids claim to exhibit the same anomaly—perhaps more a reflection of who has access to technological equipment than a true deviation. Older experiencers are four times more likely to become vegetarians than the younger crowd (even "near-death" kids snub veggies).

Afterward, parent-sibling relationships tend to be strained for child experiencers. Additionally, kids are more likely than adults to suffer socially and to report having regrets about what happened to them. An astounding number would go back to the Other Side, even if that meant suicide. Child experiencers, whether still young or grown, seldom see a counselor and receive less help when they do. This is *not* true with adult experiencers, contrary to how loudly they may contest the fact. Because the disparity between children and adults in this area is so enormous, it begs further exploration.

FAMILY/FRIEND ALIENATION One-third of the child experiencers in my study admitted to having problems with alcohol within five to ten years after their episode. Almost to a person, they claimed that undeveloped social and communication skills were the culprit, along with an inability to understand what motivated family members and friends.

Unfortunately, 42 percent of the child experiencers I interviewed underwent the tragedy of parental and sibling abuse. And note the *sibling* abuse—big brothers and sisters can pack a mean wallop or give a nasty squeeze when they're roughhousing or angry. The worst of all horrors, always, is parents who mistreat their children. While such abuse is rampant throughout the general population, the additional stresses inherent in the near-death phenomenon and its aftereffects seem to exacerbate situations that are already less than ideal.

Still, there's another aspect to the issue of alienation that, for the child, may be even more profound. Completely aside from any abuse or peer pressure from family or friends, and whether or not parents are supportive, the most significant factor is *who or what greeted the child on the other side of death.* What parent, no matter how wonderful or loving, can compare with the Holy Spirit? What person, friend or foe, can interest a child who has visited the bright realms and become buddies with an angel? For the child experiencer, connecting with such transcendent love, then abruptly losing that connection, can be very confusing, if not devastating.

THE ISSUE OF SUICIDE Children reason differently from adults. Unaccustomed to a consideration of cause and effect, they tend to act on impulse; hence the high degree of alcoholism, suicidal tendencies, and even actual attempts at suicide. It seems perfectly logical to a child that the way to rejoin the light beings met in death is to die and go back. This is not recognized by them as self-destructive. *Yet it is the children, not the adults, who are the most likely to leave the heaven of their near-death experiences and return to life so their families won't be saddened by their deaths.*

Parent-child bonding is initially quite strong. These kids *want* to be with their families. That bonding brings them back, time after time. When I interview youngsters, their common retort is, "I came back to help my daddy" or "I came back so Mommy won't cry." The parent-child bond doesn't begin to stretch thin or break until *after* the child revives. The climate of welcome or threat they are greeted with, as well as how the episode ended, directly impinges on everything that comes next.

The story of Nadia McCaffrey, now of Sunnyvale, California, gives us an example of what can drive a child experiencer to attempt suicide. While spending her vacation from convent school at her grandparents' estate in France, seven-year-old Nadia was playing in a meadow of wildflowers when she stopped abruptly. She had disturbed a red asp viper, a deadly snake. "It stayed perfectly still for a long moment, curled on its tail in a perfect circle, the upper body standing straight up, two piercing eyes staring deep into my soul. I am petrified. I want to scream. I can't move. A horrible pain suddenly flooded my senses. The snake left very fast; two tiny spots of blood appeared on my left ankle."

Nadia struggled up the steep hillside, but collapsed before her grandmother found her. First aid was immediately applied; her grandfather pedaled his bike to reach the only public phone in the village to summon a doctor. Here is her account of the crisis.

I left this dimension and was gone for about a week. It was then that I saw her. She introduced herself, saying, "I am your little mother of the sky." She was beautiful. I still see her so clearly, as though she were standing in midair, glowing with an extremely bright and powerful light, so loving and warm and comfortable. Leaving my body in my bed, I floated in her direction. She smiled very softly and opened her arms, holding up the palms of her hands to help me understand that I was not to come any closer as I listened to her. She visited me twice. Each time the message was the same and each time I did the same thing—slipped out of my gray skin.

The sight of this puffy form was unbearable to the spirit I had become.

The last time I saw her, she wore a long white gown with a cord knotted at the waist. Her head and shoulders were draped in blue material. There was a live green snake at her feet and a tear-shaped drop of blood on her right foot. Both her arms were extended toward me, with her palms up. Her head was slightly bowed, but I can't remember seeing her eyes. I wanted to curl up in her arms, to remain with her rather than return to my body, but I had no choice. My body claimed me, and I was overwhelmed by pain and sadness, and unable to completely understand what had happened to me. I had to stay in bed for a couple of weeks. My leg was three times its normal size and of the same mottled color as the snake. I refused to talk with anyone. I hated being back in this dimension. I was filled with resentment, and longed to slip out of my painful and disfigured body.

Later Nadia learned that an adult will survive for only twenty minutes after being bitten by an asp, yet she had lived for over two hours without the antidote. People said it was a miracle that she had survived. It took months for her to learn how to walk with a cane, but her spirit didn't heal as quickly. "I started asking my grandmother about the beautiful lady. I desperately needed some information about my experience. She seemed to be startled by my account, full of fear, and horrified at what I was saying. She cautioned me— 'People would not understand. They would put you away forever if you told anyone about this.' From then on, she thought that I was possessed and never let me forget it until the day she died.

"The rest of my childhood was not happy or good. I became a rebel, fighting everything and everyone. The sisters at the Catholic school I attended didn't know what to do with me. When I turned seventeen, people said I was beautiful and bright, yet no one knew I did not want to live. Although [I was] very popular, I pushed people away and isolated myself. I was not able to share the way I felt and ended up hurting people as I rejected their offers of friendship. After seeing the Lady of Light, being back was not easy. At first, I thought she would return. When she didn't, I wanted to be where she was, in the light, with the love. There was a hollow spot in a park tree where a limb had been removed, and into it I placed a statue of the Virgin of Lourdes. It comforted me to visit her there. On the wall of my grandmother's bedroom was another picture of Mary that reminded me of her and I talked to it, keeping hope alive, wishing that she would speak to me or give me a sign."

Soon after, Nadia decided to go back to the light. She made two suicide attempts. The first time, she swallowed pills marked "poison." She became very sick, vomited, lost consciousness, and was rushed to the hospital, where her stomach was pumped. Visits to a psychiatrist began.

The second time I became more sophisticated, calculating the [number] of pills required to end my life. It worked but, unfortunately, a girlfriend from the village came unexpectedly to borrow a schoolbook and she found me wearing a beautiful ball gown, with no sign of life except a feeble pulse. The hospital was forty minutes away.

I was out of my body, looking down at myself. I lost interest in nurses and doctors trying to revive me and was attracted to a long tunnel. I could see a very bright light at the end of it. I floated inside and with what seemed to be extraordinary speed, reached the light. Oh, the light, the peace, the great feeling of love. Once more I was there. Then a voice, extremely powerful, a man's voice, said I had to go back, I had work to do. Sadly I returned to my body, finally understanding that I had to stay. This experience totally changed my life. Once I knew I could not go back, I stopped fighting the world and began to pass on the love that I had once received.

Today, Nadia McCaffrey works in hospice care and is active with Compassion in Action: The Twilight Brigade,[2] a volunteer group dedicated to helping those who face death.

MONEY, MISSION, AND HOME Look at what occurs once child experiencers mature: job satisfaction 80 percent, home ownership 68 percent. Add these to those long-lasting marriages and you get a picture of contentment adult experiencers can't even begin to match, and one that the general population might envy. Maybe it's the added years, the extra time children have to experiment with what works and what doesn't as they grow up. In fairness, adults are on the opposite end of the developmental curve, with the bulk of their lives behind them. It is interesting to note, though, that salary motivates neither adult nor child experiencers, as the majority tend to eschew money and materiality, possessions, and awards. Why is it, then, that so many child experiencers put such strong emphasis on home ownership? Adults can't wait to be rid of their mortgages; kids can hardly wait to have one, and once they get a home, they keep it. Their attachment to home, I believe, is a direct result of losing their "real home" when they were children. This wound appears to create a subconscious need to make certain that no one can ever take away their home again.

Youngsters seldom do anything about their mission (the reason they believe they came back to life) until they are older, even if they know what their mission is. Adults seem almost driven to communicate theirs and mobilize necessary energies quickly. Yet it is the kids who wind up doing more and making a more positive and lasting contribution to society. Perhaps this is another finding that simply reflects the age difference, but maybe not. I have observed that child experiencers tend to mature rapidly after their episodes, while adults become more childlike. Thus, while the kids cogitate and plan, their seniors take all manner of risks and "run with the wind." Emotionally, the kids come back as the grown-ups; the adults revert to being like children.

JUDGMENT The nonjudgmental aspects of near-death episodes are touted by almost everyone, a result of the very real presence of unconditional love and forgiveness most adult experiencers report. But with children, another story emerges: many are met on the other side of death by a being whose role is that of a critical or loving parent. This parental figure either gives orders, judges them for past deeds, or in some manner prepares them to meet and fulfill their destiny by instructing them in advance on what to look out for and how to behave. Images of a critical or loving parent are most often found in cases from Asia and various indigenous cultures like that of the Native Americans, yet child experiencers from the industrialized nations describe similar "lecture" episodes as well.

There is a counterpoint to this among adult experiencers, and I would say it is the past-life review. Older children, teenagers, and adults have a lot of these—opportunities to witness or relive their past experiences in this life and see how their actions affected others. Even though some report a tribunal arrangement (with judges actually judging them for past indiscretions, errors, or mistakes), most claim that it was "me judging me." They had an opportunity to fully experience the end results of deeds and decisions so they could learn from what happened and do better in the future.

On the subject of judgment, then, the most prevalent manner of disclosure for children seems to be the instruction they are given; for adults, what they are shown. The impact of judgment, or the lack of it, strongly interweaves itself throughout what comes next in the experiencer's life.

CHARACTERISTICS TO BE ALERT FOR IN CHILDREN

- A powerful need to have a "home," even if it is only their own bedroom.
- An equally important desire to have an "altar" of some kind in their "home." Anything on the altar is holy.
- An intense curiosity about God, worship, and prayer. Many insist their parents attend church afterward—any church is fine.
- An unusual sensitivity to whatever is hurtful or to lies, especially as reflected in world events and the "white lies" parents and siblings often tell.
- Loss of boundaries, as if they have "no skin." They may have to relearn social courtesies and common rules and regulations.
- An ability to merge into or become one with animals, plants, or whatever is focused on. Borders on self-identification in multiples. Can ease back to normal self-image with age and increased socialization.

- Heightened otherworldly activity and psychic displays. Drawn to mysticism and the paranormal.
- A change in sleep patterns. May forgo naps entirely in favor of increased flow states.
- An awareness of the life continuum and anything "future," including future memory episodes.
- A shift toward being a fast talker and fast thinker, with a driving need to create, invent, read, and learn. May be misdiagnosed as having attention deficit disorder (ADD). Explore alternatives first before considering drugs.[3]
- Behavior changes in school. Just as many become disruptive as withdrawn. This can carry over into family life, with authority figures merely tolerated.

According to Diane K. Corcoran, R.N., Ph.D., a former Army nurse and leading proponent of educating medical professionals about the near-death experience and its aftereffects, especially in kids:[4] "Children may not realize that the things they are feeling are common aftereffects. They may be able to see things others don't, or they may at special times know things that are going to happen but find that nobody believes them. We need to listen to children. And we need to let them know they're okay.

"Just last week, in a workshop of nurses," Corcoran added, "a young mother said she had a two-year-old who had a near-drowning incident. She emphasized that they were not a religious family and she and her husband did not teach about God or church; however, since the incident, she said, the child has been talking about angels and wants to be one when she grows up. She drags the family to church now, and is very involved with all that happens at Sunday school. 'It's as if her angels are *personal friends,*' the mother remarked. 'What do you think is the matter with her?' Even after the lecture I gave on near-death states, she still was not sure that her daughter might be an experiencer."

HEALTH

For 73 percent of the child experiencers, aftereffects *increased* over the years. Participants were emphatic about making that claim, stating that the older they became the more exactly they fit the profile of characteristics, trait for trait. Some became ambidextrous afterward or switched handedness. A number of them showed me how their handwriting had altered, as well. Changes could be that profound! Not everyone was so affected, though. A few participants noted only slight changes and tossed off their episodes to overactive imaginations when they were young.

Intriguingly, however, I found a correlation between *those who reported the fewest aftereffects* and those who were *the most challenged healthwise as they aged*. They were the *same* individuals.

I'm not indicating here that a lack of aftereffects means poor health. Rather, what I have observed is that there seems to be a link between a childhood *repression* of aftereffects and the profusion of health problems that can occur later.

The child who is expected to be "the same as always" after a near-death event can block the experience as well as many of its aftereffects, even to the point of denial that anything so ridiculous could ever have happened. Yet all too often there is a price to pay for such repression, not only in the increased probability of health challenges when older, but also in the individual's feeling strangely empty or lost, agitated that something important seems to be missing from his or her life that can't quite be identified or understood.

Certainly, there are some experiencers who are permanently crippled or handicapped after their episodes, or are weakened to the extent that they go on to endure severe or chronic illnesses once grown. Nevertheless, the pattern of aftereffects is still apparent in most of them. Dealing openly with the impact of near-death states casts a decided advantage in how happy and healthy an experiencer can become.

Like adult experiencers, child experiencers show a preference for alternative approaches to medicine as they mature. All of those in my study who claimed now to have excellent health (77 percent) credited their good fortune to a more spiritual reverence for life, along with having turned to things like herbs, homeopathy, massage, and vitamin and mineral therapy for healing. As they aged, most found pharmaceuticals difficult to tolerate.

One particular case worth noting is that of Cheryl Pottberg of New York, who had her near-death episode at age thirteen during heart surgery. In her late thirties she suffered a cardiac arrest, which damaged her liver. She could not metabolize normal doses of heart medication, and it poisoned her system, necessitating the insertion of a temporary pacemaker. Two months later, while having open-heart surgery to correct the original heart defect, she had her second near-death experience: a reunion with her grandmother, who had been dead for thirty-three years, and a session involving "God's Word" and predictions for "the end of an age."

Millennial prophecies emerging from an adult scenario are rather common, but an experiencer as critically ill as Cheryl turning to a medical physician for help and receiving exactly what was needed via *holistic* means is nothing short of miraculous. Unable to endure further surgery, yet far from well, she discovered Gerald M. Lemole, M.D., one of the most respected heart surgeons in the country, who had shifted his practice to embrace a wide range of alternative healing techniques. Lemole is known to send patients with complex heart conditions to local health food stores *before* considering surgery. His success rate using holistic treatments is so high that it has become an embarrassment to his surgical colleagues.[5]

Part of the vitamin protocol he gave Cheryl Pottberg was the herb milk thistle, which is known to benefit the liver. Six weeks later, blood tests showed that she had near perfect liver function. Also, her heart condition has improved to the extent that she is back in college earning a degree in social work, determined to complete her mission of committing to paper "the prophecies of God."

SPECIAL HEALTH PRECAUTIONS FOR CHILD EXPERIENCERS

BLOOD PRESSURE Although more adults than children exhibit a substantial drop in blood pressure after their experience, all should be aware that current medical opinion considers long-term low blood pressure as a major component of chronic fatigue syndrome and therefore a disease that should be treated chemically. Experiencers who continue to be hale and hearty and energetic should let their doctors know that low blood pressure is *normal* for them.

LIGHT SENSITIVITY All well-meaning adults shove children outside. Fresh air is healthy. Kids need it. But if the child is a near-death experiencer and the schoolteacher or coach or parent forces him or her to practice or play in bright sunshine for long periods of time, day after day, the results could be troublesome. Because of their unusual sensitivity to light, they can be subject to allergic reactions to bright sunshine or unusual states of fatigue followed by a weakening of the body's immune system.

SOUND SENSITIVITY Peer pressure is hard for youngsters, and especially for teens, to contend with. Types of music listened to and decibel level comprise the mark of allegiance to whatever is "in." At dances, proms, parties and gatherings, even schoolwide assemblies in the auditorium, sounds are blasted out, tuned "way up" or "far out." If the teenager is a near-death experiencer, any type of loud music or noise can be painful—even injurious. Most prefer nature's sounds, classical music, or the broad range of New Age music now available.

DECREASED TOLERANCE OF PHARMACEUTICALS When a child is ill, he or she is rushed to a doctor or maybe the emergency room in a nearby hospital, where a shot is administered or pills are prescribed. This is standard procedure. But if the little one is a near-death survivor and suddenly more sensitive, possibly even allergic, to the type of pharmaceuticals normally administered to a child of his or her weight and age, the treatment can be more dangerous than the illness. Alert the physician.

The public, for the most part, is unaware that near-death states engender aftereffects or that youngsters are often affected in special ways. Thus, when child experiencers complain of strange headaches or manifest a series of colds or flulike symptoms when there seems to be no good reason for such ills, they are told, "Toughen up, kid," or, "It's just your imagination." Considering the range of their new sensitivities, the wiser course of action may be to investigate their complaints.

PHASES OF INTEGRATING
THE AFTEREFFECTS

The child you get back after a near-death episode is a remodeled, rewired, reconfigured, refined version of the original.

Whereas it takes the average adult experiencer about seven years to integrate the full range of aftereffects, it can take children twice that long. Why? Because of the extraordinary lengths they can go to to deny, ignore, or block the reality of what happened to them and is continuing to occur. Fitting back into the family of origin is a survival necessity for children. And, *whatever the family suppresses, the child represses.* Comments such as these are typical:

> I never felt free to talk about this when I was younger. People didn't and still don't believe things like this. But I know the truth, and that's what's important.
>
> *Clara Lane, Belmont, Ohio. NDE*
> *at age ten, appendicitis*

> Because others cannot accept my experience as real, I have had to keep it locked up inside me for the most part, and that creates a feeling of isolation and loneliness and of "being different," all of which is ultimately depressing. I guess the one word to describe others' lack of belief is anguish.
>
> *Carol Jean Morres, Long Beach, California. NDE*
> *at age fourteen, extreme distress in epigastric area*

> I had no childhood after my near-death experience. I felt cheated.
>
> *Beverly A. Brodsky, Philadelphia, Pennsylvania.*
> *NDE when nearly eight, during a tonsillectomy*

The process of integration, at least among those I have studied, takes place in four distinct phases. Some zip right through all four in rapid fashion, and with few distractions. Others take many more years than might seem reasonable. Each person responds to the phenomenon in unique ways. The following chart highlights what is average for most.

Brain Shift Phases of Integration Most Experiencers Go Through

Phase One | *First three years*
Impersonal, detached from ego identity/personality traits. Caught up in desire to express unconditional love and oneness with all life. Fearless, knowing, vivid psychic displays, substantially more or less sexual, spontaneous surges of energy, a hunger to learn more and do more. Childlike mannerisms in adult experiencers/adultlike behavior in child experiencers, a heightened sense of curiosity and wonder, IQ enhancements, much confusion.

Phase Two* | *Next four years*
Rediscovery of and concern with relationships, family, and community. Service and healing oriented. Interested in project development and work environment. Tend to realign or alter life roles; seek to reconnect with one's fellows, especially in a moral or spiritual manner. Unusually more or less active/contemplative. Can resume former lifestyle, but more desirous of carrying out "mission."

Phase Three | *After the seventh year*
More practical and discerning, often back to work but with a broader worldview and a confident attitude. Aware of self-worth and of "real" identity. Tend toward self-governance and self-responsibility. Spiritual development an ongoing priority, along with sharing one's story and its meaning. Dedicated. Strong sense of spiritual values.

Phase Four**	*Somewhere between twelfth and fifteenth years*
	Immense fluctuations in mood and hormonal levels. Often discouraged or depressed while going through a period of grieving—reassessing gains and losses from the experience, while fearful that effects are fading. Many problems with relationships, money, and debts. A crisis of "self." If able to negotiate "the darkness light can bring," a depth of maturity and confidence emerges that is unique to the long-term effects of a transformation of consciousness.

  * Child experiencers in my study who turned to alcohol for solace (33%) began drinking during this phase.
** Child experiencers who attempted suicide (21%) did so in this phase.

The seventh year is like a marker, a first birthday that celebrates the experiencer's ability to "bring to earth the gifts of heaven" in practical and meaningful ways. Somewhere between the twelfth and fifteenth years, maybe up to the twentieth, there is another marker—a second birthday—and it catches most experiencers unawares. *It is a second drop, a second shift.*

The second drop is like a second death, in that it heralds a time of life reversals and the need to ask some tough questions: Were the sacrifices I have made since my experience worth it? Am I capable of carrying out my mission? Is it possible to live a spiritual life in the earthplane? Have I been honest with myself? Are my aftereffects fading? If the experiencer can successfully negotiate the challenges of this second drop, a second shift is possible—a major advancement toward "the peace that passeth all understanding."

Every one of the child experiencers in my study who ever had a serious problem with alcohol started drinking during phase two—a period when relationships of varied types become primary and the pressures of pursuing further education or a job versus the need to launch their mission tend to overwhelm. As to why they drank, the majority said it was to ease the pain they felt or to escape the ridicule of their families and friends.

Of those who attempted suicide after their episodes, all of them did so during phase four. Also, most of those who had another near-death experience in adulthood had it in phase four. Example: a young boy drowned at the age of five, miraculously revived fifteen minutes later, and immediately began to "see through" people and act in "odd" ways. As he matured, what interested his agemates bored him. Behavior problems resulted. Once he turned eighteen, he joined the army, hoping he would die. He did, in an accident. He had another near-death scenario during resuscitation that explained the earlier one and gave him the courage he needed to transform his life.

The second drop that occurs is not always as perilous as it was for the young man just mentioned, but, unlike the "first birthday," this is a time of *reckoning* and *reassessment* when experiencers make major decisions that require new commitments. The first shift can be linked to the original near-death state. The second shift seems more dependent on choice, on the experiencer's willingness to surrender to a greater plan. Regardless of how integrated and spiritual an experiencer may appear to be after the seventh year, all pales by the power unleashed *if* the second shift occurs.

MUTUAL PARENT-CHILD EPISODES

Occasionally in my work, I have come across cases where both a parent and that parent's child were experiencers. Some of these parents openly shared their accounts with their families and were especially sensitive to the needs of their child experiencers. Most, however, were not this communicative, nor did they attempt to determine if their children might have had near-death experiences, too—*even when it was obvious* that a child could have. Sons and daughters, then, were often left to fend for themselves without benefit of the guidance and understanding their parents could have provided. Two such cases follow.

L. S. Gordon had her episode at the age of three during a tonsillectomy. Like typical child experiencers, hers was the Initial type. She never labeled her episode growing up because it wasn't as detailed and experientially complex as descriptions she had heard of her mother's. She and her mother never discussed this. Forty-seven years later, she was finally able to reexperience her own scenario's radiance and allow all of the aftereffects to manifest, due to the manner in which her mother died. As she tells it, "Bette Gordon, like an NDE Medicine Woman, with intent calm, was reading Betty Eadie's book *Embraced by the Light*[6] when she suddenly propped it up in the crook of her elbow, looked at the book, and exited. Incredible! She died with the reassurance that what she had always known was true." L. S. Gordon wrote a book-length manuscript of poetry as a way to reconcile what had happened to her. An excerpt:

> *If we could see as God does,*
> *we might find legions of angels surrounding us,*
> *legions of souls upholding us, learning*
> *from us, humbled and amazed*
> *by what we dare. Do we lose hope sometimes, give in*
> *to fears that make us monsters? We do: To bear*
> *the dense, particulate fruits of this world,*
> *we must be capable of anything.*

The second example is that of Michael and Ralph Kelley of San Antonio, Texas. Ralph, Michael's father, contracted typhoid fever at age thirteen. The illness was so bad that when his ordeal was over, he had to relearn how to walk. During the high fever, he experienced a scenario that so overwhelmed him that it shaped the rest of his life. Although his legacy was the Light's Perfect Love, which he showed in the caring and forgiving way he treated people throughout his many years, he never discussed his episode until just before his death, when his son Michael insisted that he "'fess up." It was important for Michael to hear his father's story, since he had also experienced a near-death state when he was just two years old. He had opened the car door during a family outing and had fallen out, suffering a brain concussion and other injuries.

According to Michael: "I distinctly remember watching from outside of my body as my father picked me up from the street and put me in the car. I also remember a city bus stopped in traffic and seeing a brilliant white light that seemed to surround everything." Michael often revisited the scene in his mind. "My school grades always suffered because the message from those replays was more profound than anything offered by my teachers." Another car accident and brain concussion in adulthood brought on a second episode. Afterward, Michael was so shaken that he lost control of his life. It wasn't his father, but near-death research, that finally made an important difference for him. Yet since he confronted his father, Michael has been more in touch with the truth of his own experience.

Why life? We live to execute a properly conceived life plan whereby each human being becomes an artistic genius. The LIGHT's knowledge and love are the paint and the inspiration that we, God's little brushes, apply to Earth's giant canvas, allowing each of us to add our few, unique brush strokes to God's Grand Painting of Life.

In both of these examples, the children went through needless periods of confusion because their parents, for whatever reason, never invited dialogue about otherworldly journeys—neither their own nor those of their children. What happened in these two families underscores the fact that just because one has shifted to a more loving and spiritual way of living does *not* mean that new reality is translated into every aspect of one's life.

Those who have undergone a brain shift/spirit shift still make mistakes and ignore, without meaning to, the very loved ones most in need of their understanding and their care. This happened to me with my own children, and I've seen the same thing occur with ever so many others.

SIX

MANY TYPES,
ONE PATTERN

Probably a dozen times since their death I've heard my
mother or father, in an ordinary, conversational tone of
voice, call my name. They had called my name often
during my life with them . . . it doesn't seem strange
to me.

Carl Sagan

Just as there are many ways in which one can undergo a transformation of consciousness, numerous are the types of conditions that can trigger a near-death state. Whether the initial
experience can be recalled or not, the pattern of aftereffects
remains the same, and what occurred is recognizable *more by
that pattern* than by any memory of the episode. The reason is
straightforward: the aftereffects validate the phenomenon.

Two particular aspects of this are rather curious: how a
near-death experience can occur *without* the individual
being clinically at risk of dying, and how an experiencer can
display the aftereffects pattern, yet have no recall of a near-
death scenario. By taking a look at these factors, we can gain
a better sense of how truly widespread the incidence rate of
the phenomenon has become and how dynamic its reach.

WHEN NOTHING THREATENS

It is possible to have a near-death experience that has as great an impact and the same patterning of aftereffects as the worldwide phenomenon, *and not be in the throes of physically dying.* No one can explain why this occurs; we just know it does. Officially, the research term for the anomaly is *near-death-like experience.*

How many people have had such an episode? Well, in 1992, the International Association for Near-Death Studies discovered that, of the 229 experiencers attending their annual conference that year, 37 percent had their episodes in settings unrelated to anything that could be construed as life-threatening.

Children have near-death-like experiences, too, especially after they have formed concepts of death that are meaningful to them and pondered the question "Can I die?" I've noticed that powerful shifts in their awareness take place once they consider this. Many go on to dream about dying afterward; some have nightmares. Similar to minirehearsals, a child's death dreams can actually be healthy explorations of mortality. There are times, though, and always without provocation or warning, when a simple death dream can suddenly escalate into a deeply involved experience resembling near-death, and *with the same far-reaching consequences.* The three dreams that follow illustrate this.

According to Margaret Evans of Roscoe, Illinois, the night before her seventh birthday was a life changer. She and her twin sister were sound asleep in the same room when, for no apparent reason, Margaret sat bolt upright. Actually, only half of her did—the half that projected out of her body. "I looked straight at this being of light just a little off to my left but in my line of vision. The being generated the white-gold light I was bathed in—a very soothing, accepting, loving light. It was very bright but not hard on my eyes. The angel was neither male nor female and had no distinct features, just the sense of them. Communication between us was telepathic. My first thought was a remembrance that this moment had been prearranged between us before my birth. It was an opportunity for me to leave this life if I so desired, and the angel was there to offer me that choice. To my right, coming out of the light, were my dead grandparents. They seemed to be on the other side of a doorway. I knew they were there but I couldn't see them. I wanted to go to them so badly. I was happy about the reunion waiting for us, but then I turned and somehow saw my sister and myself still asleep in bed. I thought of my parents in the other room and how I would miss them if I left. They would be very hurt. I decided to stay."

Margaret claims that as soon as she made the decision, the

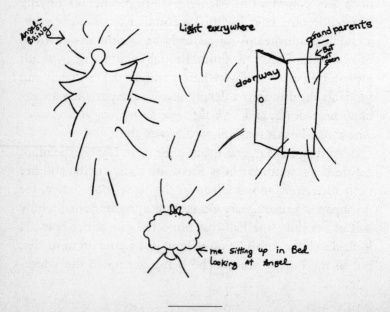

angel told her she would live a long life and then disappeared, along with her grandparents and the light. Never once did she regret her decision to stay, as "the angel and my deceased grandmother have protected me throughout the years since."

Muriel E. Kelly of Chandler, Arizona, had rheumatic fever at age six and was left with a serious heart murmur that necessitated a lot of bed rest. At the age of twelve, still very sickly, she fell into an unusually deep sleep when suddenly, "I found myself standing on a cobblestone road with people around me dressed in bright robes—red, blue, pink. Everything was so bright and sunny. Birds were singing. Baby angels were smiling and flying around. I saw all different sizes of angels. The music was hauntingly beautiful."

Hearing her name called, Muriel turned to see Jesus beside her, dressed in a white-and-red robe. "He knelt down and gave me a hug and I hugged him back. He told me we were going somewhere to talk. When he held out his hand, I noticed the hole in the middle of it from the nail." As the two walked along, people nodded and smiled, and children played. "When we arrived at the building, we went inside and walked on a red carpet to a throne where Jesus let me sit on his lap. We talked and he let me hug and kiss him. He had long brown hair, brown eyes, a wonderful voice, and skin darker than mine."

Jesus told Muriel that someone was waiting for her, so the two walked out the door to the street and over to an apartment with many doors, laughing all the way. He told her she would know which door to knock on. As he watched approvingly, she found a door that seemed somehow special. A voice inside beckoned her to enter. It was her mother, who had died when Muriel was nine, leaving behind five children. Their reunion was love filled. "I asked Mama where Daddy was, and Cecil, Willie, John, and Paul. Mother told me they weren't here 'cause it wasn't their time. I had no idea what she meant, so she took me to an area where we sat on a cloud and looked over the whole world. My mother located my dad and brothers riding in a car. We could see right through it. Dad was driving, and we heard my brothers and Dad crying, saying, 'I wish Muriel was still here. We miss her. If she were here we wouldn't be mean to her.' My dad said I was in heaven with Mama and I'll never be back. I didn't know what was going on. I started crying for my dad and brothers. I remember really sobbing and wishing I was back with them. Well, I got my wish. I woke up in bed."

Muriel healed completely soon afterward, and went on to live a normal life. She even passed the navy's physical when she enlisted—*no heart murmur was detected, nor has any trace of her early health traumas ever reappeared.* Her doctor is as surprised about this as she is.

Tom Meeres of New Jersey was fourteen when, on a summer night, his peaceful sleep turned into a terrible fall through a spiral or tunnel. He had had falling dreams before and had experienced a similar sensation under anesthesia, so the thought "here I go again" was of some comfort—yet this "dream" was to be unlike anything before or since.

Falling was fast; he heard undulating noises and garbled voices. He slowed enough to recognize that the tunnel walls were ribbed, but the falling continued until he became nauseous. Just as he wished for death to stop the terror of it, he suddenly found himself in a velvety dark void, feeling totally supported and cared for. He curled up in the fetal position, but panicked with the thought that this isolation might last forever. No sooner did he think that than he discovered he was in a dark cave. "To the right is a beautiful light coming from a round opening above me. I am drawn in and through the light until I find myself looking out over the sheer drop of an immense cliff." Fear struck once more, but the light helped him float, then fly: "I'm high above a strange landscape with a river valley that seems to stretch out forever. The light suffuses everything so that forms are discernible only in shades of gray. All fear is gone and there's just a wonderful lightness of being. I am myself, yet there is no feeling of separateness from the light."

Sensing a city and people beyond his view, he wondered who they were and what they were doing. He noticed his arm as he flew toward them, expecting to see a shadow. There was none, for light shone everywhere. Before he could think of a question, his grandparents appeared before him. "I can't tell you what they look like or how I hear them, but they say who they are, that they care about me, that I must go back, that I have a purpose. I don't want to go. They strongly urge me to, and I agree." As he turned around, he recognized that he had gone too far. The openings in the cliff were too numerous to count, and he couldn't tell which one he had emerged from. Getting back became a struggle, like swimming against the tide. He started

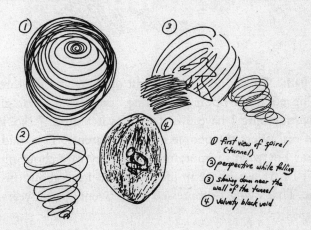

① first view of spiral
   (tunnel)
② perspective while falling
③ slowing down near the
   wall of the tunnel
④ velvety black void

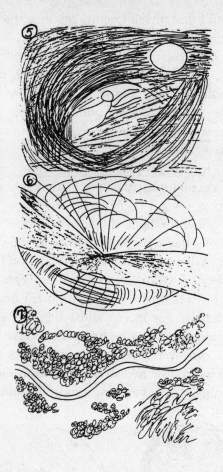

to panic. Finally, he saw the right opening and fell through. "The euphoria upon awakening," said Tom, "was greater than anything I have ever felt. Was it a dream? No, it was too real. Were the people my grandparents? They said they were, but what's important is that they care about me and that I have a purpose in life. Who can I tell about this? No one. That's why I suppressed it for twenty-seven years."

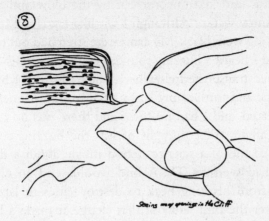

Stains may openings in the Cliff

Other types of conditions can foster a near-death-like experience. Here is one that involves a blow to the head during a rock fight; another concerns a tumble down flights of stairs, as well as a "visitation" from a ghostly dog.

At the age of ten, Timothy O'Reilly of New Jersey happened to get caught in a rock fight between two groups of kids. The empty lot where the fight occurred was long and like a big pit, with swampy water about a foot deep at the bottom. To cross the swamp, Timothy had to negotiate a walkway of wooden planks laid atop discarded tires that zigzagged through high weeds. Three-fourths of the way across, the opposing group began throwing rocks at him.

"I started to run back to my friends," explained Timothy, "but when I was about ten feet from dry land I looked up and saw this kid holding a huge rock over his head. I think the rock was about the size of my ten-year-old skull. As he let go of it, I remember thinking, 'This thing is going to hit me.' I turned my head to the right just before the rock hit me square in the back of my head."

He was knocked unconscious by the blow and fell into the swampy water. "Although I felt like I was still standing, everything went black. My arms were stretched out to either side and I heard a buzzing sound. I couldn't see my body as it seemed transported elsewhere, but I had one. I began to flail back and forth as my legs started to sink or melt. They disappeared, and I had no torso and there was no gravity. I wasn't afraid. All I thought of was the buzzing sound. It reminded me of a science-fiction movie about a dinosaur that I had seen on TV. A bird would send an electrical charge from his long beak to destroy cities in Japan, and whenever the bird sent out that charge, it made a buzzing sound like the one I experienced. Later, I had to go to the hospital for a few stitches."

Round Trip, the touching forty-minute video that captures the transformations undergone by people who have had near-death experiences, is the creation of Timothy O'Reilly.[1] He never connected his interest in the phenomenon with what happened to him as a child until he researched the video. Filming *Round Trip* did more than assist him with recall; it seemed to be the stimulus he needed to release long-suppressed aftereffects. "I had a spiritual growth spurt doing the project," he chuckled, "and all kinds of intuitive flashes and synchronicities occurred. They haven't quit."

Laura Hanner of Redding, California, was at her wits' end at age thirteen. She had been repeatedly raped by a close family member, yet when she asked her alcoholic mother for help, she was beaten and accused of lying. Upset, she fell down five flights of stairs in the apartment building where she lived. "I do not remember how I ended up at the bottom of the stairs. Somehow I did. As I was sitting there crying, I became aware of this clicking sound. I looked in the direction of the sound and saw a dog coming to me. He was built like a German shepherd but as white as snow. That dog came up to me, sat down, and spoke via mental telepathy. *He spoke to me in my head.* It scared the heebie-jeebies out of me. I did not know what to think, but I was spellbound. He told me that I would never again have to feel fear, and that I was going to be watched over from then on. Well, I was astonished. *Dogs don't talk.* But that one sure did!"

Afterward, Laura, who had been failing in school, suddenly excelled, with new and exciting ideas flooding into her mind day and night. People seemed to come out of the woodwork to protect her whenever she needed them. The appearance of Space Dog, as she called her mysterious visitor, signaled a complete change in her life. "I am just a little four-foot, ten-inch Puerto Rican woman. Ever since Space Dog, I've had visions and they come true. I'm not trying to impress anyone, and I have nothing to gain by making this up. It happened."

Laura's talking dog did *not* act like a mental projection or a hallucination. He behaved as if he was a messenger of hope from the Other Side, who validated her sense of worth while inspiring her to transcend the poverty of her life.

Near-death-like experiences defy the reference points established in near-death research. But the fact that *they do match the overall pattern of the near-death phenomenon,* both in experience types *and* in their aftereffects, demands that we entertain new possibilities of thought.

A particularly exciting possibility is that perhaps death is auxiliary, *not causal,* to the phenomenon. Perhaps the real orchestrating force of near-death and near-death-like states is that of the soul as it journeys through the human condition, making course corrections along the way, revamping and revitalizing itself whenever necessary.

TUCKING IT AWAY

"The incident is probably my most vivid memory, and I can 'play' it back step by step, without change, as I did when I was a young child. It is doubtless the most profound and distinct experience of my life." Larrick Stapleton of Wynnewood, Pennsylvania, spoke those words. He was only four when death came to call, and he's in the minority. Not because he died and had a near-death episode, but because he has never forgotten it. Children are *six times* more likely than adults to tuck away their experience, lest it interfere with the demands and expectations of growing up.

Because of this tendency, child experiencers are subject to recurring dreams or nightmares about what happened to them, or such behaviors as an excessive need for attention or privacy, reckless activities as if they had a "death wish," or a haunting sense that something's missing.

For instance, Amanda Csanady of Glenview, Illinois, does *not* remember having had a near-death episode when she was two and a half. Her mother was informed six hours after she was rushed to the hospital that she had suffered a febrile convulsion caused by an ear infection. Her ear troubles necessitated numerous surgeries over the years that followed, finally reversing her 40 percent hearing loss. Today, she is an active young woman who happens to exhibit the profile of brain shift/spirit shift aftereffects.

Her mother sent me a collection of her childhood drawings, which are full of rainbows with tunnels through them and mysterious yellow doors leading to secret places. I have included a sampling of her artwork to show how effectively children can communicate the deeper truths of their lives *without words.*

At the age of three and a half, a year after her brush with death, Amanda drew a picture of her family. Shown are Mom and Dad, her two older brothers, and to depict herself, a small, featureless nonentity as yellow as the nearby door and barely visible in the middle placement. A contemplative white sun, outlined in yellow, shines from the upper right. (Note how she sees herself: not all there, still part of the secret worlds behind the door, the sun unable to help her.)

At four and a half, as a kindergarten assignment to make placemats, Amanda did another drawing. The faint, almost invisible door is on the left this time, with a happy self-portrait in the middle. On the right, there is a small rainbow with a tunnel through it. All three central figures are suspended in air and outlined in yellow. (Note a richness of detail, showing she is adjusting to her life, but still connected to and part of the otherworld readily available through the mysterious door.)

My Family

At age seven, she won a Fun-velope contest held by Mead Johnson. Her drawing was used for the month of June in their 1987/1988 Enfamil calendar.[2] A tunnel leads into the large rainbow on the right; perhaps the pool has one too (both are suspended). The train-track sidewalk goes to the far right from a rainbow door on a happy red house filled with windows. There are a canopy of hearts, much yellow, many details, and the sun, finally full-strength and at the upper left. (Note lavish, uplifting elements and a bright sun where most children draw it, upper left. Lots of yellow, but only behind structured outlines. Although mysterious openings abound, the picture illustrates a joyous return to family bonding and the confines of earth.)

Amanda's use of yellow and the imagery she drew is significant. Youngsters who have undergone near-death scenarios invariably tend to picture themselves as Amanda did—as a featureless yellow nonentity, and often with a mysterious yellow door nearby—until parent-child bonding is

reestablished. When I ask children about this, they usually shrug, smile, and say, "It's a secret." Additionally, I have been privy many times to drawings done by children shortly before they died. Not only did their artwork depict fore-knowledge of their coming deaths, but the majority *drew the continuance of their lives in yellow*—as streamers, bubbles, cir-cles, wispy clouds, or butterflies, winding upward to the left-hand corner of the paper, *where they had told their parents God was.* (Remember Amanda's sun? It was strong and bright *only* at the upper left.)

The color yellow is an important aspect of near-death states in general. In those cases where a light is seen during the experience, kids and adults alike usually describe it in terms of yellow–gold–white, with yellow predominant initially, as if it were a kind of filter or lens.[3] Interestingly, yellow, as a color in the light spectrum, cannot be seen or captured on film directly. Since there are no color cones for yellow on the human retina, for us it is a product of brain chemistry. In photography, it emerges from the chemical processing of film images. One way or another, yellow results from chemicals. Considering the force of its light during near-death states *and* transformations of consciousness, I suspect yellow heralds extraordinary accelerations of chemical activity in the brain proper—another clue to the validity of the brain shift/spirit shift theory.

Amanda Csanady's drawings, then, along with her peculiar use of yellow and the fact that she displays the aftereffects pattern, convince me that she had a near-death episode at the age of two and a half . . . irrespective of "missing memory."

People like Amanda are *nonexperience experiencers,* those who claim nary a glimmer of memory about anything so exotic as a near-death experience, yet live out their lives as if that's exactly what once happened to them. This situation is especially pronounced among children.

Here is a brief presentation of four such cases, of adults trying to make sense of why they have always been oddly different from their fellows.

Debi Canon, Fair Oaks Ranch, Texas. "Died" at age ten months during surgery on a tumor formation in the nervous system that had left her paralyzed from the waist down. Her death was expected; her survival wasn't. "I grew up 'knowing' there was something special about my being alive. I knew I had a specific job to do, yet I resented being here and being denied my 'assignment.' People thought I was weird. They would nod and change the subject whenever I was around. I was unusually intuitive, could read minds and see into someone's soul. I had a strong sense of being guided to where I was needed." Debi's IQ tested out at the genius level. She has an abstract mind, a master's degree in nursing, is proficient in science, and has "healing hands." Animals seek her out. She is like no one else in her family. A homeowner with a long-lasting marriage and no particular regard for money, she is exceptionally healthy and totally devoted to spiritual growth and learning. The older she gets, the more pronounced the characteristics become that would identify her as a child experiencer. As her "mission," she is actively integrating spiritual healing into traditional medicine.

Randi, California. Serious health condition at age six weeks, not expected to live. "Growing up I always knew that God was real. From my earliest memories I felt very close to God. As a child, I would talk to God frequently. When I needed comfort I would picture myself in God's lap and feel secure. I have never had a good relationship with my mother. She has always treated me coldly, as did my brothers. My father was distant but there if I needed him. I felt as if I did not belong in my family. Until the ninth grade, I struggled academically in school. I couldn't seem to learn as fast as the other children. Then it was as if a light went off in my brain and learning became easy and fun." Randi had a serious case of eczema until she was fifteen, when it finally cleared up. Her mother used to say that she was allergic to her own skin. She has since begun using herbs and homeopathic remedies. Randi is a homeowner with a long-lasting marriage and no interest in money. She has an unusually bright, intuitive mind with enhancements in math and a love of history. She had "trauma-memory" nightmares as a child. She is a natural at interpreting dreams and sensing the future. She looks much younger than her years, has a glow about her, and exhibits electrical sensitivity and what she calls "gifts of the spirit" (the spiritual extension of psychic abilities).

Virgil Rinquest, Montana. "Died" at age 6 months after being suffocated by his older brother. "I started having psychic experiences as a young child. I remember loving to see rays of light coming through the door window and imagining that the light took me to Jesus. My guardian angel was always helping me. I felt connected to strangers and would walk down the street 'sending' love to people I never met. A beautiful white dove landed in front of me while I was praying once. That kind of thing often happens to me." Virgil was both religious and spiritual at a very early age and eventually became an ordained minister. There were more instances of sibling abuse from his older brother, making life difficult for him. He endured four decades of traumatic nightmares, all linked to his "death" as a child. He is a homeowner with a long-lasting marriage. Money does not motivate him; a deep desire to help others does. Missing any math and music enhancements, Virgil did receive a Ph.D. in psychology and is fluent in numerous languages. He has a quick and agile mind, is highly intuitive, and remains to this day in communication with angels. The ethereal messages he claims that angels give him enable him to balance his double career of minister and psychologist. He looks younger than his years and is currently writing a book for African American men like himself, concerning how to handle conflict successfully and heal the wounds of racial discrimination.

Sandra S., Los Angeles, California. Received too much ether during a tonsillectomy when she was nearly five and "died" of the pneumonia that resulted from the surgery. "People commented on how smart I was. I learned to read right after my experience and was reading books beyond my chronological age. I was a 'whiz' at math and spelling. Elementary school was lonely; I felt different, probably because I was too smart and overweight. Animals seek me out when they're injured and I can heal electrical things, too, except watches—they don't last. I love mythology and had a facility for languages, but I gave up the idea of becoming a mathematician or a linguist to study comparative religions. That satisfied me for many years." Sandra involved herself in Christian doctrine when young but converted to Judaism after experiencing Shabbat (the day of peace and completeness). She felt she had "come home." After one divorce, she married a child survivor of the Holocaust, and now teaches in a Jewish community. A homeowner who has been married a long time, she finds money utterly distracting. Considered a genius with "tons of energy," she wonders if her eating disorder is the result of having blocked out what happened to her during the tonsillectomy.

Nonexperience experiencers such as those mentioned are a growing phenomenon. Considering the 70-percent experience rate estimated for children by Melvin Morse, M.D., and today's increasingly efficient resuscitation techniques, it is highly possible that near-death episodes in childhood far outnumber those among adults.

With this in mind, I offer the following eight clues that might be helpful in identifying child experiencers, irrespective of what they do or do not remember.

1. A life-threatening illness or accident sometime during childhood, or an unusually stressful delivery at birth.
2. Behavior changes immediately after this incident: becoming appreciably more somber or gregarious; exhibiting increased intelligence or a hunger for knowledge; tending toward abstractions and a maturity beyond one's age; having an intimacy with God or otherworldly companions; acting aloof or estranged from most family members and friends; suddenly more sensitive or allergic; disinterested in activities "normal" for one's age group while drawn to topics like history, mythology, and language or math and science; infinitely more creative and inventive; vivid psychic and visionary displays, an awareness of future.
3. If still young, doing nearly everything earlier than age-mates. Driven to draw or write poetry about other

worlds, other realms, other ways of looking at things beyond what would be expected for the child's age.

4. Evidence of a learning reversal once in school; having to
go from abstract thinking on the conceptual level back
to concrete, practical details on the physical level. This
can confuse or threaten teachers.

5. Drawn to anything that feels like "home," and will tend
toward homeownership *even if* money is scarce.

6. Motivated by service to others or somehow making a
contribution to the greater good, rather than getting
rich. If married, apt to stay married.

7. While maturing, the profile of brain shift/spirit shift
characteristics (in chapter 2) fits better and better, as if
the aftereffects are on the increase or expanding.

8. An inordinate attraction to material about near-death
states and to people who have had such experiences,
combined with a sense or feeling that something important is missing in their own lives or somehow forgotten.

Morgan J. Blank of Pleasant Hill, California, is typical: "I
have been searching for thirty-three years to try and understand why I am the way I am. There were many times when
I felt I was crazy or delusional. I knew that the *experience* I
had when I drowned in our family pool at the age of two
affected me. It has affected the way I view the world. It has
affected the way I view people, humanity, love, our purpose
on this planet. It has affected me down to the core of my
being and on the cellular level. It has affected every aspect
of my life and I never knew why . . . *I just knew!*"

Sooner or later, as in the case of nonexperience experiencers like Morgan J. Blank, the power of the near-death
phenomenon tends to reassert itself. Spontaneous recall is
common. One man was simply surfing the Internet when

he happened upon an account that caught his eye. In an instant, a memory of his own experience returned to him, complete with those aftereffects he had managed to repress. It happened so fast and with so much power that he fell off his chair.

As children age, full recovery of their episode (be it near-death, near-death-like, or nonexperience), and the subsequent integration of the many aftereffects into their daily lives, becomes paramount. The majority turn to God for the assistance they need, or ask their angel friends for guidance. Others initiate rigorous programs of study and self-analysis, while a few practice specific yoga breathing techniques that they claim help them to surface the dormant aspects of themselves. For those who go to therapists, counselors, psychologists, or psychiatrists, benefits or lack thereof have a lot to do with the professionals' sensitivity and training.

The difficulty both child and adult experiencers have with professionals relates more to prevailing notions of what is culturally acceptable than it does with the judgment factor of whether or not the experiencer is mentally or emotionally fit. Lily Tomlin, the famous comedian, used humor to focus on this disparity: "Why is it when we talk to God we're said to be praying, but when God talks to us, we're schizophrenic?"

Sometimes an experiencer is lucky enough to find a therapist who is also an experiencer. When this happens there is instant rapport, and miracles follow. On one extreme, I know of people who were involuntarily committed to psychiatric hospitals simply because they exhibited the normal aftereffects of the average near-death survivor. A few were later released when a new therapist assigned to their case, who happened to have had such an episode, recognized "who" they were.

Those professionals who consistently have the best record working with experiencers are the ones trained in transpersonal psychology.

Joseph Benedict Geraci, an adult experiencer who is now an administrator of the New Britain School System in New Britain, Connecticut, wrote a Ph.D. dissertation titled "Students' Post Near-Death Experience Attitude and Behavior Toward Education and Learning."[4] He made some comments in his proposal that are pertinent: "Transpersonal psychology addresses those human experiences that take consciousness beyond the ordinary ego boundaries of time and space. Experiences include unitive consciousness, cosmic awareness, mystical experiences, and maximum sensory awareness."

Transpersonal psychology, as a legitimate field of understanding and exploring varied states of mind, is by its nature geared to experiencers. Other ways to "touch" memory are also effective, including art therapy, vision quests, philosophical counseling, and consciousness coaching.[5] Reconnecting the heart with the mind, not just "remembering," is the true goal.

SEVEN

CASES FROM HISTORY

> Only those who can see the invisible, can do the impossible.
>
> *Thomas Jefferson*

Powerful subjective experiences are the outworking of a force capable of causing life-changing aftereffects. The strength and intensity of this force determines the experience. And this force is spirit and spirit is real. How we respond confers value and meaning.

When spirit intervenes, it is physically felt. Some describe this intervention as a sudden "bolt of light," akin to an electrical charge. Others report a calmer energy like a force field that glows with a brilliance unique unto itself. The energy is always powerfully present, and the association made is usually to that of a light that is alive, intelligent, all-knowing, and all-loving. The very young who encounter the Darkness That Knows use similar terms—"sparkle," "shimmer," "pulsate," "radiate"—describing a soft, inviting "bright dark."

Thus, the presence of spirit is perceived as that of a *force*.

What effect might incidents like this have had on the history of civilization? Have any of these child experiencers, once they matured, made a significant impact on society? My answer to both questions is a resounding *yes*.

While the near-death phenomenon has not been noted historically in the phenomenon's now-familiar vernacular, what is recorded does offer tantalizing hints that many of our revered historical figures may indeed have experienced near-death episodes that presaged their greatness.

Use the following guidelines, as well as the eight clues suggestive of how to recognize a child experiencer given in the preceding chapter, to identify such people.

- *A serious illness or accident between birth and age fifteen that nearly claimed the individual's life.* Any record of an otherworldly vision or dream connected with the event will be highly unusual, unless he or she lived in a "primitive" social structure.
- *Marked differences in behavior afterward.* The subject may be ahead of or different from agemates for that historical period, becoming more so as the years advance, with a nontraditional or nonconformist attitude. He or she may be possessed of a charm or charisma that attracts people, animals, etc. He or she could be considered socially retarded when young, yet unusually creative and bold; unafraid of death; highly intuitive; aware of things future.
- *Presence of the cascade of aftereffects.* Although it is difficult to find existing records that register such characteristics, personal letters, journals, and even poetry can reveal a great deal. Electrical sensitivity seldom applies, but a unique sensitivity to the sun, sound, and the types of medication used at the time are often noted. Be alert for excessive complaints about stomach upsets, numerous colds, or serious bouts with the flu. Even though most are

blessed with robust health, increased sensitivities, allergies, and occasional fits of depression may have made
health issues a concern.

- *An almost obsessive drive to accomplish a particular task or project.* Most will have been workaholics with no sense of
  time or money, yet inclined to have property or be
  aligned with distinctive places or groups, whether or not
  they ever married.

Using these indicators, it is possible to find historical per-
sonages who so closely match the profile of aftereffects and
behavior characteristics that it is extremely likely they
underwent near-death experiences as children.

Most of the saints in the Catholic Church had their first
experiences of God as children, and many conform with the
indicators. Great visionaries and prophets of all persuasions
often match, as well.

For a specific example of perhaps a quintessential child
experiencer, consider Abraham Lincoln.[1]

When he was a child of five, Lincoln fell in a rain-swollen
creek and drowned. His older friend Austin Gollaher
grabbed his body and, once ashore, "pounded on him in
good earnest." Water poured from Lincoln's mouth as he
thrashed back to consciousness. Although there is no record
of the young boy's confiding an otherworld journey to anyone, ample remarks were made by friends and family who
observed his sudden craving for knowledge afterward, his
insistence on learning to read, and his going to exhaustive
lengths to consume every book he could find. Five years
later, just after his mother's death and before his father
remarried, he was on a wagon driving a horse and yelled,
"Git up," when the horse kicked him in the head. He hov-

ered at death's door throughout the night, with his sister Sarah in attendance. On reviving, he completed the epithet aimed at the horse: ". . . you old hussy." Little more can be gleaned about the incident until, as an adult, and referring to himself in the third person, he is quoted as saying, "A mystery of the human mind. In his tenth year, he was kicked by a horse, and apparently killed for a time."

Among the characteristics suggestive of a brain shift/spirit shift that Lincoln came to exhibit: the loss of the fear of death, a love of music and solitude, unusual sensitivity to sound and light and food, sensing in multiples, wildly prolific psychic abilities, a preference for mysticism over religion, absorption tendencies (merging), dissociation (detachment), susceptibility to depression and moodiness, increased allergies, regular future memory episodes, hauntingly accurate visions, the ability to abstract and concentrate intensely, clustered thinking, charisma, moral upliftment, a brilliant mind, perseverance in the face of problems and obstacles, and a driving passion about his life's destiny.

Certainly the argument can be made that Lincoln's many idiosyncrasies were the result of his extreme poverty as a youth coupled with a relentless determination to succeed. Yet nothing during his early years indicated genius; none of his unusual talents appeared until *after* he had survived two close brushes with death. As an adult he nearly died again, and once more he displayed signs that he might have had yet another near-death episode—with additional aftereffects.

Similar patterns can be observed in the lives of Albert Einstein, Mozart, Winston Churchill, and Black Elk.

A Lakota Sioux, Black Elk witnessed the Battle of Little Bighorn and participated in the Battle of Wounded Knee. But that's not why we know of him. He is famous because a white man by the name of John Neihardt interviewed him in 1930 and 1931, and forever captured his visions in the singular triumph *Black Elk Speaks.*[2]

Black Elk first began to hear voices and see spirit beings coming from the clouds as early as age five, but this confused him and caused many complications. At age nine, however, he fell seriously ill, his legs and arms swollen, his face puffed up. A disembodied voice spoke to him: "It is time. Now they are calling you." Two men appeared from out of the clouds, holding spears that flashed lightning. "Hurry," he was told, "the Grandfathers want you." With that, he left his body behind and flew away into the cloud realms, joined by the men he "knew" were Thunder Beings.

The imagery in this, a full-blown Transcendent near-death experience, is among the most spectacular I have ever come across: flying horses, flaming arrows, forests, mountain peaks, cloud realms, explosions of color, beings of various types. Featured in his scenario are the Six Grandfathers (great powers), who taught him many things and both told and showed him his future, which would include hard times ahead for his people and special powers he would be given to help them. Then, his mission was revealed to him: he must *save the world* (a pretty tall order for a nine-year-old). Astride a bay horse and from the highest of mountains, he gazed upon the whole of the world he was to save and saw more than he could tell and knew more than he could ever say. All knowledge was his.

Beings he "knew" as the Riders of the Four Directions came to him and he saw in a sacred manner the spirit shapes of all things, and he knew that all people must live together as one people. "And I saw the sacred hoop of my people was one of many hoops that made one circle, wide as daylight and as starlight. And in the center grew one mighty flowering tree to shelter all the children of one mother and one father, and I saw that it was holy." A spotted eagle took him back to his home and became a lifelong "messenger" for him.

"I could see my people's village far ahead, and I walked very fast, for I was homesick now. Then I saw my own tipi, and inside I saw my mother and my father bending over a sick boy that was myself. And as I entered the tipi someone was saying: 'The boy is coming to. You had better give him some water.' Then I was sitting up and I was sad because my mother and my father didn't seem to know I had been so far away."

Black Elk remained as if half-dead for twelve more days. His experience replayed repeatedly in his mind, but he could not share it. If he tried, "It would be like a fog and get away from me." Too young to understand, he felt like he no longer belonged to his people. Feeling himself to be a stranger, he hardly ate and longed to be back in the spirit world.

Black Elk began to hear voices and have visions on a regular basis, including warnings of troubling times in the future. A medicine man recognized a powerful light coming from him. He seemed to levitate at age thirteen as he was prepared by his father for the Battle of Little Bighorn. By age seventeen, he was warned in a visitation from the Thunder Beings that a penalty of death by lightning would be meted out if he didn't share what had happened to him when he was nine. He finally told his story to a medicine man, who arranged for the whole tribe to make costumes and then act out each element of his story in ceremony, to benefit the whole tribe. Realizing that saving the world really meant healing people, he became a medicine man and began to heal the sick.

Black Elk was very much aware that it was not he who cured people, but the Great Spirit. This humility lasted throughout his lifetime. He lived a rather active and colorful life, but in the twilight of his years and nearly blind, he became a recluse. His conversion to Christianity was a mere convenience, for he knew that God was the God of all. Biographers were discouraged from writing about him, as it was against federal law at that time for Indians to discuss Old Ways or the religion of their past.

Nevertheless, John Neihardt, who was familiar with the Lakota Sioux and was accompanied by his interpreter, Flying Hawk, went in search of Black Elk. Why the old man was waiting for him as if he was expected, and then broke federal law in trusting this white man and sharing with him his greatest vision, is a mystery—until you know something about Neihardt. At the age of eleven, Neihardt had "died" of a high fever and had a dramatic near-death experience. Never the same again, he became as Black Elk . . . one of those who *know*. The recognition and camaraderie between the two were instantaneous, and they became as family. Published in the thirties, the book Neihardt wrote went out of print but was rediscovered by Carl Jung and republished in the sixties. It became a best-seller and has sold well ever since, hailed, even by Native Americans, as the Rosetta Stone of authentic Native American spirituality.

A less familiar name, perhaps, is that of Walter Russell.

He had his first near-death experience at age seven, and it prepared him in a strange way for the financial disaster his family would soon suffer. In 1881, at age ten, Russell was pulled from school and sent to work, keeping "a good heart" because of the unfailing faith he had gained from his otherworld journey. A musician since infancy, he secured a church organist position at thirteen and thereafter became entirely self-supporting and self-educated, earning his way through five years of art school. When he was fourteen, his plans were interrupted by black diphtheria and another near-death episode, in which he was officially pronounced dead by an attending physician. He claimed to have discovered the secret of healing during this event, as he felt he had entered into "at-one-ment" with God.

These two near-death experiences set the stage for dramatic periods of illumination that would occur every seven years throughout Russell's life. According to Glenn Clark in his biography of Russell, entitled *The Man Who Tapped the Secrets of the Universe,* "He escaped encyclopedical educational systems of information-cramming and memory-testing which filled other children's lives until they were twenty-five. He used his precious youth to find out the secret mysteries of his inner Self. His whole life has been used in the search of the real Self and the relation of this real Self to the selective universe of which he knows himself to be a vital part."

Russell excelled in whatever he turned a hand to, and won lasting friendships and lucrative art commissions. He had a studio in Carnegie Hall in New York City, became a commissioned sculptor for President and Mrs. Franklin Delano Roosevelt, was a longtime friend of Mark Twain, and painted and sculpted Thomas Edison. Walter Russell's motto was "Mediocrity is self-inflicted. Genius is self-bestowed." At age forty-nine, he suddenly was enveloped within the fullness of cosmic consciousness. This state lasted for thirty-nine days and nights without abating. "My personal reaction to this great happening left me wholly Mind, with but slight awareness of my electric body. During practically all of the time, I felt that my body was not a part of me but attached to my Consciousness by electric threads of light. When I had to use my body in such acts as writing in words the essence of God's Message, it was extremely difficult to bring my body back under control."

Once he regained use of his faculties, he set about to record the experience in *The Divine Iliad* and then spent six years penning *The Universal One,* a text containing the drawings and revelations given to him of the universe and how it worked, covering such subjects as chemistry, physics, and electromagnetics. He later corresponded with Albert Einstein about his own theory that this is a "thought wave" universe created for the transmission of thought. His second and lasting marriage was to English-born Lao Russell, herself a visionary since childhood, who grew up knowing she was here "to change the thinking of the world." Together they established the University of Science and Philosophy and published many books, including a home-study course on spiritual principles. Although both have long since passed on, the University continues their work in offices located on Afton Mountain, near Waynesboro, Virginia.[3]

A final example is Valerie V. Hunt, Ph.D.

Very much alive, although retired, Dr. Hunt was the very first researcher to objectify electronically the aura of light around people, places, and things, which, she showed, does indeed exist and has specific color frequencies that register consistent and measurable waveforms. I have seen some of the films taken of her experiments, especially those of the human aura, showing how it expands and contracts according to mood, attitude, and interactions, and I can attest to the impact these films have on people—entire crowds have been moved to tears. To actually *see* the electromagnetics of aural energy fields play out right in front of your eyes is an awe-inspiring privilege. Her work is a scientific milestone.

Her early years were rather difficult, though. She was in a coma at the age of three, with dire predictions for her survival. Not until she was an adult working in the field of psychotherapy was she able to revisit that harrowing time and recover her childhood near-death experience, complete with the sensory world she had once known. Considered a mystical child by her mother, she early on had a reputation for being so far ahead of other kids that most avoided her. She escaped by composing poetry, drawing, singing, and thoroughly indulging in the spirit realms around her. Before the coma she had been an outgoing, exuberant child. Afterward, she became serious, quiet.

According to Hunt:

> One day, quite by surprise, my parents took away my paints, my paper, my crayons, and my books. No one wanted to hear about the fun things my mind created. My frustration mounted daily—my world had rejected what I found exciting. I mumbled to myself angrily with little satisfaction. My parents didn't listen. Finally, I started "multiplying words" with God, for real. I flashed back to my months in a coma when I experienced being with God in a beautiful land of flowers, sweetness, and love; quiet serenity. I wanted to stay forever, but I recalled that God had said I would go back to the world to bring it beauty. I complained because I did not like the world, and besides I had no talents for beauty. I was just a little girl who sensed beauty but didn't know how to create it. I remembered God assuring me that I would be given ample talents to do my "beauty work." It was then that I became aware of people, the room, and things I had known before. I had returned from my distant journey.

At first, adults praised my pictures and writings, expecting I would grow to be an artist. But also I sensed that despite my new gifts, the world wanted me the old way—a little, ordinary girl, doing what normal little girls my age did. It was then that I hid in a deep, dark hall closet . . . where I sat feeling quite protected, so that I could argue with God. I knew it was all God's fault. He had pushed me out of Heaven, given me skills that no one would let me use. In spite of my anger, God was kind and understanding with a new solution—if I couldn't bring beauty, I could bring knowledge.

Hunt continued, "To this frightened, angry little girl in a dark closet, the answer seemed strange, although also sustaining." Hunt expresses a common lament of child near-death experiencers when she says, "Although I had been enthralled at my post-coma skills, there was also a haunting suddenness to my change that was scary, particularly when adults said that it was not 'real.' "

Her full story, and her twenty-five years spent as one of the foremost researchers in the science of human energy fields, is chronicled in her book, *Infinite Mind: Science of the Human Vibrations of Consciousness.*[4] As director of the electromyographic laboratory in the physiological science department at the University of California, Los Angeles, and as a researcher in the shielded "Mu" room of the physics department, she was able to document scientifically the light, color, and sound of "invisible" energy networks and how they relate to human health. She evidenced what psychics see and healers sense, as well as the common perceptions of those who have undergone a brain shift/spirit shift. She explored the energy patterns of light and spirit, and proved them real.

I have no doubt that history is replete with stories such as those I have just relayed. What happens to children is significant, for it directly engages evolution's nod. Our science, art, culture, our discoveries, and the multitude of decisions and acts that make up our history, all are profoundly affected by little ones who flit around the edge of death's curtain, then return, forever different.

Raymond A. Moody, Jr., is now convinced that the near-death phenomenon itself is a primary factor in stimulating the growth of culture throughout the ages. He bases his finding on the fact that the entire tradition of intellectualism in the West can be traced back to sixteen men, among them such scholars as Pythagoras, Democritus, Socrates, and Aristotle, and that eight of the sixteen had experienced a near-death or out-of-body state. Records exist that suggest all sixteen used a single near-death experience as a central model in their formulation of the concepts for matter, reason, and truth.

Moody currently publishes a newsletter that goes into detail about these sixteen men, as well as other aspects of near-death research, including what he calls "the empathic death experience."[5] He has found that bystanders, be they loved ones or medical personnel, can "co-live" an individual's death in the sense that they can subjectively join in consciousness with the dying to help escort the individual into the light, perhaps experiencing elements of departure that may mimic the classical pattern of a near-death state, and/or sharing in some indefinable way the power of forgiveness and love. Moody feels that once people realize how easily they can participate in life's fullness, and make a profound difference in their own lives and the lives of others by doing so, there will be a spiritual revolution like nothing the world has ever seen.

EIGHT

EVIDENCE FOR A LIFE CONTINUUM

We are all islands in a common sea.

Anne Morrow Lindbergh

When does the soul enter the body?

Most traditions claim at first breath.

But what if that's wrong? Challenging the age-old assumption that first breath heralds the entry of the soul are both a recent medical discovery and an observation I made while interviewing child experiencers of near-death states.

The medical discovery is that the fetus at twenty-six weeks, or six months in gestation, can feel and respond to pain like an infant. This means that surgery on fetuses and newborns or, for that matter, third-trimester abortions, can no longer be performed without consideration of the pain threshold and welfare *of the new life,* not just those of the mother. Nor can physicians and religious leaders continue to justify withholding anesthesia for newborns during circumcision; the excuse "It's traditional" is now null and void.

In my study, I observed that prebirth memories usually began at around the sixth or seventh month in the womb, with fully one-third of my participants having such memories still intact years later. Recall of the actual birth event was commonplace overall, although greater detail was given by experiencers born prematurely or exposed to trauma within three months of birth.

Some had recall as a fetus earlier than month six, even of their conception and of actively taking part as a spirit in choosing their own DNA. Most of those who spoke of remembering their conception, however, said they "floated" in and out of their mothers' wombs until finally "settling in" when fetus formation was more complete.

Thus, medical research of fetal awareness and responses to pain *directly overlap* with the period when the majority of children in my near-death research reported the beginnings of memory *as a soul resident within a human body.*

This unexpected link suggests that by the third trimester the fetus has a developed consciousness with faculties in place—that it is an inhabited body undergoing the final touches necessary before birthing from a water world to one filled with air. How we regard and treat a fetus, therefore, has less to do with mother or medicine than with how we feel about the reality of spirit.

Most birth and prebirth memories are clear and coherent, yet will quickly fade or be repressed if the child, once verbal, is ridiculed or silenced when expressing those memories. If child experiencers are allowed to be themselves without pressure, doors to their world swing wide open. What they say may seem senseless unless we remember that, with kids, *how they feel* about what they perceive matters more to them than any logic or imagery. Most of what they report, though, is not only accurate but startlingly mature, *as if they, as souls, were comfortable with leaving and reentering* a life continuum *existent beyond that of the earthplane.*

The idea of a life continuum, of life before birth and after death, has been broached repeatedly. Here's what I noticed in twenty years of research about the varied aspects of this most important of all mysteries.

CHOOSING TO BE BORN

Not everyone I interviewed who had birth or prebirth memories claimed to have had a choice in the process of leaving where they were to come into form, but the majority did. I examined the adult case of Berkley Carter Mills in *Beyond the Light* to establish a sense of how experiencers tend to remember this. He was "killed" attempting to load compressed cardboard into a truck at his job. His life review, conducted by Jesus, started at conception. An excerpt:[1]

> He relived being a tiny spark of light traveling to earth as soon as egg and sperm met and entering his mother's womb. In mere seconds he had to choose hair color and eyes out of the genetic material available to him, and any genes that might give him the body he would need. He bypassed the gene for clubfootedness, then watched from a soul's perspective as cells subdivided. He could hear his parents whenever they spoke, and feel their emotions, but any knowledge of his past lives dissolved.

In the same book, I also spoke about Alice Morrison-Mays, who has become something of a celebrity for giving public concerts in her home despite dealing with the pain of emphysema and a collapsed adrenal system (Addison's disease).[2] Besides near-death states, she could also recall prebirth memories, but chose to remain quiet about them until now.

Alice remembers operating from the viewpoint of the soul in deciding which parents to choose before incarnating. A candidate for family that resonated with her was a musically gifted couple who were eager to have another child after having lost a baby son soon after his birth three years earlier. Feeling especially welcomed by them, she made the choice to be their child and basked in joy and anticipation for most of the nine months. "About the time of my birth, my peaceful and happy gestational existence was shattered. I found myself being 'hit' with and immersed in terrible shadow and dark mistlike clouds. The impact of this gave me sudden pain and despair. I seemed to be swimming in agony. I didn't want to go on with the birth but I couldn't return to where I had come from."

The death of Alice's maternal grandfather was the cause of the problem. "The unexpected shock of it was a blow to my mother, who absolutely adored her father. She suppressed this shock, along with the depths of her grief. What she 'held in' hit me with full force. She was determined not to express her feelings because of her fear that doing so would jeopardize the birth of her second child, now at full term. An additional impact on me was the medication the doctor gave to hold off my arrival. So, in effect, I received a 'double whammy' and was lost in the trauma of it all. Four days later, birth was forcibly induced, and with great reluctance I was born, apparently in good health."

Alice believes that her mother's decision to suppress grief directly affected her in her unborn state, leading to, on the positive side, an unusual emotional sensitivity that helped in her career as a symphony cellist, and, on the negative side, a rare and severe form of emphysema that was genetic in composition and crippled her slowly.

EMBRACING A BIRTH AFFLICTION

Arvin S. Gibson, in his paper entitled "Near-Death Experience Patterns from Research in the Salt Lake City Region,"[3] wrote about the case of a young man named DeLynn who was told during his near-death episode that he, as a soul, had chosen to be born with a debilitating disease. Quoting DeLynn: "The specific choice of cystic fibrosis was to help me learn dignity in suffering. My understanding in the eternal sense was complete—I knew that I was a powerful, spiritual being that chose to have a short, but marvelous, mortal existence."

But with Christina Moon of Eureka Springs, Arkansas, the issue of choice differs. She had two near-death episodes: one stemming from the emergency cesarean section performed on her mother (she was too large for a natural birth and "got stuck"), and the other at three months of age during plastic surgery to correct a deformity (she was born with a harelip and cleft palate). "I had an angel around me all the time," Christina recalls. "She passed her finger over my mouth before I was born and left me with my harelip. But I never felt anger about it because I was always aware of her love for me." Christina received the "gift" of a handicap without complaint but has no memory of actually choosing it. She harbors no regrets about it, as the compassion she has gained from dealing with her deformity has become a tremendous advantage for her in hospice work and midwifery.

LETTING THE MOTHER KNOW

Expanding on the idea of the child remembering life before birth, it is a well-known fact that women throughout the world who are about to become pregnant typically either somehow meet their baby's spirit in advance of conception or dream about their child early on in what is termed an announcing dream. This phenomenon has been investigated by numerous researchers over the years, among them Robert L. Van de Castle, Ph.D., an expert who authored *Our Dreaming Mind*.[4] The consistent accuracy of these announcements implies that the soul is not only capable but also interactive when making itself known.

N.T.A. of Omaha, Nebraska, provides us with an example. Now an adult, she experienced a near-death scenario at age thirteen months when she bit an electrical cord. "With my first pregnancy, I knew it was a girl. She came to me in my dreams several months before conception, a totally wonderful nature girl who loves the outdoors. With my second pregnancy, sunshine came shining through and a boy spirit appeared in my mind. I heard him say, 'I'm here.' " A mother from Portland, Oregon, offered: "Before my last child (a daughter) was born, I saw her twice, once in a small child's body, looking at me, and once right after her birth, as a wonderful sort of butterfly-shaped light flash—extraordinarily beautiful and bright." She continued, "The whole mental state of pregnancy is one big altered state of consciousness. It's like a *'near-life experience'*—you get a little peek behind the veil."

REACTING TO A CHANGE OF PLANS

How does one explain toddlers who detail in graphic terms their mothers' attempts to abort them when they were still in the womb? Or little ones who inform their parents that they chose to kill themselves *while still babies* because they didn't want to stay here? Yes, I have encountered many such cases. Here's one that incorporates both extremes.

Dorothy M. Bernstein of North Olmsted, Ohio, had a total of four near-death events, two in childhood and two as an adult. Her childhood accounts centered around the cessation of breath *because of her choice to die*. Today, we would say that she was a victim of sudden infant death syndrome, or SIDS. But her understanding of what happened to her is quite different from how we might interpret it. She claims, "I knew the truth about how my mother tried to abort me, and even again at five weeks before I was born, me, the seed of an alcoholic, a rapist, an adulterer, an abuser. Who could blame her?" While still a virgin, her mother had been raped. Dorothy, as a fetus in the womb, said she was aware and knew all that had happened. "I never cried as a young child. I remember being wet and hungry and thinking, 'Don't cry or she'll kill you.' My mother thought I was such a good baby, but I remembered the pain."

Dorothy noted that her crib was kept in her parents' bedroom after her mother married. One day, at the age of ten months, she witnessed some sexual behavior she was not meant to see and was punished by her father. She can vividly recall the painful confusion that preceded her decision to "go home," and then knowing exactly how to kill herself: by expelling all the air from her lungs and constricting her chest muscles to make her heart stop. Her last remembered thought was, "Oh, God, how could he hurt me like that?" and God's mysterious reply, "Perhaps he was trying to protect you." As she explains it, that "voice" so startled her that she gasped, which restarted the breathing process. Her account is filled with descriptions of a brilliant light, focusing on the mirror's reflection of an angel picture, having a spirited dialogue with a tiny person perched at the head of her crib, and promising God: "I will never forget from whence I came, nor will I ever deny you."

Nonetheless, at the age of three and a half, badly traumatized by the neglect and abuse she received from her mother after the birth of her mother's "love child" (her half-sister), she recalled once again making the decision to "go home." She used the same method, with the same results. Only this time, Dorothy said, feelings of warmth and love coming from the crown of her head convinced her that God wanted her to live and to help her sister. Breath returned, but, sadly, the situation with her family worsened. When I spoke with Dorothy about her two bouts with breath stoppage as a child, she mentioned reading a newspaper article about sudden infant death syndrome. "The doctors suspect the infants die because they just forget how to breathe. Not true! *I chose not to breathe!*"

Sally Dunn, a grandmother from Gila, New Mexico, gives us another way to view "a change of plans." "My daughter Jennifer's first child, Sashena, drowned at eleven and a half months. Jennifer 'knew' Sashena would not be here long. Very unusual day when it happened. The soul returned in her brother, Jasper, four years later." Sally noted that Jasper seemed to be in a hurry to grow up, yet he made strange sounds. "I puzzled over the sounds for months and then, Aha!, realized what it was. It was the noise a person would make when trying to close off passages to water coming in through the nose and throat. I knew Jasper would stop making those noises once I told his mom, and that's what happened." When Sally shared her revelation with Jennifer, she had one of her own. "Mom, when you had an abortion, that was the same soul that was in Sashena and is now in Jasper."

REMEMBERING PAST LIVES

The plan of the soul seems to encompass multiple dimensions of existence, as well as countless lifetimes. Children speak of this as casually and confidently as they might inquire about dinner. What follows are a number of accounts from my files.

The father of five-year-old Gregory Buxton of Montreal, Quebec, tells about his son's close call at birth. "Gregory did a loop loop in his mother's womb and got the cord tied around his neck. Every time he would try to come through the birth canal, the cord would tighten and he would retreat back into the womb. When he was finally delivered, he was blue and unmoving for quite some time. Today, Gregory looks at people with a depth of love that is inexplicable. He claims to remember heaven *and* past lives. He told me in detail how he had been a fighter pilot during World War I and had been shot down in Europe. He went through his death, telling me how long it took him to die because 'there weren't any doctors around.' He told me how he had lived in New York in an earlier life and that he had hung around his present sister before her birth so, through her, he could experience where we were living in Brooklyn. He said he was disgusted to see how New York had gone downhill since the day when he last had lived there."

Margaret Evans, a near-death-like experiencer, explained: "I have no memory of being inside my mother; neither does my twin sister. Just previous to birth, I was very high up above the planet with other spirits. There was quite a group of us and although we couldn't 'see' each other, we all knew we were together on a mission. A terrible thing was about to happen on earth that could not be stopped and we were needed to help out." Margaret described seeing a gigantic mushroom cloud coming toward them in the sky, a cloud

that meant instant death to many people, and recalls how busy she and the other spirits were, assisting the dead in "crossing over." Years later, she finally learned what had occurred—it was 1945 and atomic bombs had been dropped on several cities in Japan. She remembered dying before the mushroom cloud incident, as a little girl of about five or six in a small village in England. "I was riding in the front seat of a car with [a man] who seemed to be my uncle. He was speeding and lost control. We slammed head-on into a stone wall. The split second before impact, I shot out of my body. I was very happy with the family I had then and wasn't supposed to die as young as I did." In her present life, she was frustrated as a child to discover that the father she had now looked similar to her previous father in England.

Rhona Alterman-Newman of Cherry Hill, New Jersey, who was pronounced dead at the age of six months after surgery for a strangulated hernia, began having past-life memories as a youngster. Feelings of horror and fascination were often triggered, for instance, when she was driven past a large stone mansion that stood between her two grandparents' homes. "I could 'see' kids playing outside on swing sets and seesaws. I'd tell my parents this and they would tell me to shut up. I knew it was an orphanage. I knew the layout of the house, and I could 'see' a green tiled bathroom. Either my little brother, or I myself as a little boy, got hung in there. My older sister in this life was there, too. I contacted one of my grandmothers and asked her about the house. She said it wasn't an orphanage, but I insisted. It took her a long time to find out that in the late 1800s it had been a Jewish orphanage. None of us could have known that."

Denise Grover of Lansing, Michigan, recounted, as so many parents do, that "because of rather stifling religious limitations, I had no concept or belief system to accommo-

date ideas about reincarnation. However, my son Neil, at the age of three, began that introduction. While sharing a meal with myself and his older siblings, Neil boldly announced, 'I was dead before, but now I am alive again!' We all found this amusing, to say the least, since there appeared to be no context for it. But, for years, he maintained that he had been here before. At about the age of eight, Neil would wistfully express an interest in seeing pictures of how he looked before. No, not the baby album photos, but he would voice his desire to know what he looked like the last time he was here. By nine, Neil explained to me how the idea of parallel universes works. Additionally, he often dreamed (and still does) of events that play themselves out in the near future (future memory). He is an impeccable judge of a person's character, seemingly 'seeing through' facades with ease."

ENCOUNTERING THE UNBORN

If the cases I have submitted thus far seem beyond evidential credibility, here are two that demand serious attention.

Four-year-old Jimmy John drowned in his parents' backyard swimming pool. He was an only child. His mother was in her late twenties, his dad in his early thirties. Emergency crews arrived within minutes. CPR was administered. Nothing happened. Fifteen tension-filled minutes later, the professionals managed to resuscitate the boy. His distraught mother, beside herself with relief that her precious son was back among the living, suddenly turned chalk-white as Jimmy John blurted out for all to hear, "I met my little brother. He's 'over there,' where I just was, and he told me all about Mommy having him pulled out of her tummy when she was thirteen." The boy went on to correctly detail

his mother's secret abortion, an event she had never discussed with anyone. In fact, she had long since forgotten about it. Jimmy John was absolutely elated to discover he had a brother; their reunion had been laughter filled. Both vowed to remain in contact now that they had finally met. Neither parent could handle Jimmy John's report of his newfound sibling. Embarrassed, frustrated, confused, and horrified, his mother nearly had a nervous breakdown. His father, feeling betrayed by his wife's secret past, sued for divorce. Jimmy John's joy was lost in the shuffle, as was the communication I had established with the family. How this incident resolved itself, I do not know.

Children's near-death scenarios that feature the youngster being greeted by an *unborn* sibling, as happened to Jimmy John, are *not* that uncommon. In most cases the unborn were either miscarried or aborted, and the amount of time that has passed seems to make no difference. But, occasionally, the unborn are *future* siblings yet to be conceived. The next story is one such episode.

Merla Ianello of Thetford, Vermont, recalls that as a child she saw a guest in her home who was about three or four years old choke to death trying to eat a plastic-wrapped frozen juice treat called an Ice Pop. She insisted on naming them "Death Pops" after that, and one day she asked her mother who the child was. Her mother, staring in disbelief, said, "It was you." Merla remembers standing in the kitchen doorway looking into the dining room when the incident occurred. "My mother was screaming and shaking a kid upside down by the ankles. My father was leaning over, helping her. My younger brother sat in a chair at the table, watching. *I was so scared!* Boy, that kid must have been really naughty. I would never be so bad as to make Mom shake and scream like that! She yelled *my* name. I cringed and was upset that maybe I had something to do with her anger. Before I knew it, my mother took away my Ice Pop and my brother Lou washed it down the drain. I wanted to protest but was too scared to ask for it back. She might get mad again and this time shake *me* by *my* ankles." Merla witnessed this episode from several feet *outside of her body*. Guilt prevented her from associating "the kid" she saw with herself. The extra child in her drawing (to the right of her mother's shoulder, indicated by an arrow) she unmistakably identified as her brother Michael, whom she could clearly see, even though her mother insists that this was impossible, as *Michael wasn't conceived yet*.

SEARCHING FOR THE "MISSING" TWIN

From the very beginning of my work, experiencers have pulled me aside and whispered things like, "I'm not all here. There's another one of me. I have a twin, but my twin doesn't have a body." This "missing" twin was occasionally a participant in prebirth awareness states or during a near-death scenario at birth and died shortly thereafter. Sometimes individuals did not discover that a twin had ever existed until years later when that twin appeared in a near-death episode of theirs. Hardly anyone will speak openly about the subject. Because several "twinless twins" filled out my questionnaire, in addition to those who submitted to interviews, I feel that I must tackle the subject of the "missing twin" phenomenon.

Although it is unconnected to near-death research, the story I am about to relate is typical not only to what I keep finding but to the discoveries of other researchers, as well. A woman (who requested anonymity) had an abortion after discovering she was pregnant. Shortly afterward she learned that she was still pregnant. Unbeknownst to anyone, she had been carrying twins—one was removed but the other remained. The woman took this as a "sign" that she must keep the second baby and raise it, so she refused another abortion and later delivered a healthy baby girl, who grew up a fast friend of her invisible twin sister. This camaraderie exacted a heavy price for a number of years, as the mother, fearful that her daughter was going insane, took her to one psychiatrist after another for evaluation. Nothing abnormal was ever found. Currently, the two sisters enjoy each other's company by communicating telepathically and through dream states. The mother has finally accepted that she has two very real daughters: one with a physical body, and the other with a spirit body.

Regardless of how we might choose to understand this story, the fact is that more and more late-term diagnosed twins are vanishing—some within hours of birth. These are not just sonogram-pictured babies, but little ones whose heartbeats and body sizes were physically monitored and accounted for throughout the entire gestational period. The absent twin sometimes disappeared without a trace, and sometimes an empty placenta was born along with the single survivor. The medical community has no explanation to offer mothers demanding answers.

A contemporary theory is that the sudden disappearance of evidence of a twin in an advanced pregnancy is proof that the fetus must have been abducted by aliens. Amazingly, there exist toddlers much too young to fancy such things who describe in detail the lives of their other halves as they grow up aboard spaceships.

Caryl Dennis has explored this area for many years. She has interviewed some 130 people involved in multiple births, the missing twin phenomenon, and UFO contacts. Her self-published book, *The Millennium Children,*[5] delves into a broad range of issues that suggest the degree to which today's youngsters are changing in behavior, ability, and temperament. Although Dennis's research protocol leaves much to be desired, what she discovered is well worth considering; her conclusions are similar to my own about kids who had near-death episodes.

In her book Dennis presents case histories of twins who have vanished early in the mother's pregnancy as well as just before birth, and she describes the empty feeling of the woman after the disappearance of a pregnancy. Of special relevance, though, is what happens to the surviving twin. Most go on to actively dialogue with their "other" (whether that twin is in spirit form or believed to be living among aliens), and, according to Dennis, they display unusual talents, faculties, and intelligence enhancements, and become creative thinkers.

Just as near-death children (and often the separation from and loss of a twin is part of a near-death scenario), single twins deal with aftereffects that can confuse, disorient, or frighten them. Even in the most tolerant of families, the idea of an ongoing relationship between the dead and the living can create schisms that result in the surviving twin's being institutionalized as mentally ill.

Dennis points out that some therapists are now specializing in this field, and that there is a magazine called *Twins World* for twins in general and a newsletter called *Twinless Twins* for singles who are attempting to deal with the grief of losing their twin and the driving need they feel to find him or her so they can be whole again.[6]

I have found that missing twins occasionally befriend or function as spirit guides for relatives besides their surviving singles. One of the participants in my research experienced an incredible healing when the dead twin of her son returned in spirit form to help her. Robin H. Johnson of Plymouth, New Hampshire, is the mother. She had three near-death episodes—the first at age two from drowning, then one during a health crisis at age twenty-three, and the third during surgery at age thirty. Of the three, the childhood incident had the greatest impact on her and set the stage for how she would face the challenge of growing up.

Recalling the event, Robin winced. "I didn't talk about the pain of almost drowning, because I was too excited about having just seen Jesus. But when I began to tell my mother about seeing the movie of my life go by, she froze like a statue. Then she said, 'That must have been some movie, Robin, as young as you are.' I think she thought I was trying to get out of having been bad. I shouldn't have been near the drop-off, the part of the river that abruptly became deep. I had made a mistake, but I wasn't a liar.

"I suddenly felt so alone," Robin continued. "I could not communicate to her. She didn't believe me. She actually seemed embarrassed that someone would hear me, like I really had lost my mind. I felt abandoned. For the second time that day, I felt terror. Who was I? Where was I? Her sternness was a warning to me that I had better drop the idea of ever sharing that I thought I had seen life from a different perspective."

Robin was assailed with guilt and fear after this experience and fell into a habit of denial that would result in self-betrayal, the total distrust of her own inner knowing. "My journey out of denial and into my full awareness of my connection with the Divine came after a spiritual awakening when I was thirty." And that awakening was her third near-death episode, preceded by the "appearance" of her son's deceased twin, Sarah.

"It wasn't until I met my nonphysical daughter, Sarah, that I learned that her purpose for being in my life was to teach me to have unequivocal trust in my intuition, my knowing." In this case, it was not the surviving twin who formed a relationship with his deceased sister, it was the mother. By communicating with Sarah, Robin was able to reclaim what she had lost at the age of two and heal herself.

EXPRESSING "SELF" IN MULTIPLES

What happened to Robin Johnson is an unusual twist to the missing twin phenomenon. Here's another one. Frank Henniker, also of New Hampshire, has to this day a vivid prebirth memory involving his twin that led to "both of them" being hit by a car and experiencing a near-death scenario when four years old.

According to Frank: "Life for my sister Cynthia and I, though quite unconfirmable, began as two eggs, not one. The outside world's vibrations made my sister want to abort before we were recognized as existing. Our parents did not get along and the water we lived in was constantly invaded with negative energy. I was told that I could not leave, by a voice known to me as Eros Thor. Eros and I had been together before. Not having the option my sister wanted, I pulled her inside me. We literally became twins in one egg. At six months in the water, we were hit by our daddy. This was confirmed before our mother died years later."

Frank's memory is of being born as two beings in one body: he and his twin sister, Cynthia (a name he has always called her). To please a violent and demanding father, *the two created subpersonalities*—twenty of them by the age of four. They were unsuccessful in their attempt to win their father's approval by appearing to be "other people," and their mother at last intervened for them and kicked the man out. Even though only one body existed, the twin duo of visible and invisible siblings referred to themselves as "we" until that fateful day around the time of their parents' last fight.

"It was a bright, sunny March day when Cynthia found an opportunity to end what she perceived as her own life. She took the body into the street, where a car ran over us with its rear tire, spinning us like a top. Witnesses said we went the height of a telephone pole and landed on our back. The body remembers the pain that came from landing spread-eagle, the bones shattering, and the skull bursting on the pavement."

Frank described a lengthy near-death scenario that included a struggle between the two siblings. Cynthia remained long enough to help him revive in "the body shell" and then disappeared. Cynthia was not a "created personality" in the sense of the subpersonalities they *together* created, a psychological phenomenon known as dissociative identity disorder (D.I.D.), formerly called multiple personality disorder (M.P.D.). From the beginning, the two existed as two and interacted in a manner now recognized as typical for twins. They *knew* each other, even as cells were dividing in the womb to form the body they would eventually cohabit. *And they took part in the cell division process consciously, actively, and from the awareness level of developed minds.*

This is congruent with the cases of near-death survivors who had full knowledge and full memory of having chosen the life they were about to have *before conception*—their parents, their genetics and characteristics, their actual birth, and the basic tendencies of the personality self—and were participants in the act of their own creation. These experiencers knew, absolutely knew, that the self they really were was the "higher self," and that they as a soul were eternal and motivated to take on life in the world of matter to learn certain lessons, experience contrast and change, and fulfill a mission of greater import—to help make the world a better place. Almost in chorus, they claimed that the biggest mistake people make during their sojourn on the earthplane is to think that they could ever exist separately from the Source of All Being. "Aloneness," they said, "is a joke our Soul plays on us so we will fine-tune the gift of free will."

Frank Henniker's case adds a new dimension to our understanding of twinning and the complexities of missing twins, not to mention the dynamics of birth and the miracle of cocreation. It also introduces the topic of multiple personalities and how the mind can defend itself through the process of dissociation. A research bulletin from the

Institute of Noetic Sciences featuring the article "Multiple Personality—Mirrors of a New Model of Mind?"[7] offers the intriguing idea that what has previously been treated as a *dis*order could possibly be the emergence of *new* order. Rather than splitting off, the mind is becoming more adept at manipulating consciousness; it has learned how to switch into different gears.

To be fair, D.I.D. child experiencers confront serious challenges, such as the conflict between the love they find on the Other Side versus the absence of love in their lives on this side, compounded by questions of trust and truth telling. (Like experiencers of any age, they tend to lose basic self-defense cautions until such time as they are able to reassess their life and its purpose.) Positives usually outweigh negatives, however, as in the case of P. Ann Baillie, a D.I.D. from Michigan.

Baillie had two bouts with death before her first birthday and experienced a near-death scenario each time. Even though being sent back to her mess of a family felt like a betrayal to her, she has this surprising commentary to offer: "I believe that the near-death experiences had a profound effect on the multiplicity. The level of fragmentation that I developed may have been a result of being unable to let go of my 'core self' and let her sleep [while another personality took over] the way many in my situation have done. I was unable to give up, even in times when surrender may have been a good idea. I also think that the near-death experiences have made conventional therapy largely ineffective for me. While I have an enormous capacity for anger, I have little for hatred and tend to pity those who abused me, much to the confusion of people around me. I have little ability or desire to relive the past, often a prerequisite with therapists who treat D.I.D. It feels like enough for me to acknowledge and honor it, but I don't seem to abreact [release psychic tension by acting out] the way many multiples do."

Baillie speaks tenderly about the universal love she encountered during her near-death episode and how the memory of it has helped her break through the barriers she had to erect in order to survive her youth. What was once a nightmare has given way to a sense of unity and inner strength, with a steady decrease in her personality fragmentation.

TAKING A SECOND LOOK

Can science tell us anything that might shed some light on prenatal awareness?

Well, we know that the recognition of language begins in the womb, not in the nursery, since sounds and voices register early on, and continuously, for the fetus. Geoffrey Cowley wrote about this research in his article "The Language Explosion." He noted, "Babies just four days old can distinguish one language from another."[8] *The Secret Life of the Unborn Child* details the pioneering work done by Thomas Verny, M.D., that led, in the early eighties, to the breakthrough revelation that the fetus makes decisions that require conscious thought, sucks its thumb, hiccups, and responds appropriately to any given stimuli, especially the emotional state of the mother.[9]

Add to this research the remarkable work of psychologist David Chamberlain, Ph.D., author of *Babies Remember Birth,* who clinically hypnotized young children and discovered that they possessed pre- and perinatal awareness as newborns and were fully cognizant of their inherent selfhood at birth despite the lack of anatomical maturity—which refutes the notion that birth memories are fabrications or guesswork.[10] David B. Cheek, M.D., a retired obstetrician and past president of the American Society for Clinical Hypnosis, continued the quest to determine at what age a baby is aware, and he found evidence to suggest that by the time a woman realizes she is pregnant, the embryo is already aware of her and her surroundings—indicating that awareness may begin at conception.[11]

Concerning reincarnation, the most notable authority on the subject is Ian Stevenson, M.D. His meticulous research on this topic is the world's best; his books *Twenty Cases Suggestive of Reincarnation*[12] and *Where Reincarnation and Biology Intersect* are unparalleled as objective examinations of the phenomenon—and what he has uncovered is stunning. Many since Stevenson have also come forward with credible material underscoring the phenomenon's validity. Of the newest offerings, the one most relevant to our discussion is Carol Bowman's book *Children's Past Lives: How Past Life Memories Affect Your Child*.[13]

Because there is such a high rate of pregnancies that have been diagnosed as twins but resulted in only one birth, most doctors dismiss the vanished "other" as having been claimed by nature's efficient "waste disposal system." The thinking is that fetuses that may have been damaged, malformed, or incomplete are either absorbed by the healthy twin or resorbed by the mother. All of the obstetricians I interviewed about this felt that the exceptional incidence of twin loss was "no big deal." The mothers who suffered such a loss disagreed—many were distraught.

Two major national debates have brought the issue of missing twins to the forefront. These are the abortion conflict and a growing concern, even among the mainstream populace and credible researchers, about alien abductions. The question I must ask differs from those addressed by either debate: In cases where there is a verifiable death of one twin, why do so many surviving twins report having an ongoing relationship via spirit with their other halves? This question deserves serious attention.

The fact that people can remember their births, have awareness in the womb, see the unborn and the missing, remember past lives, alter destinies, and interact with the living or dead has inspired new fields of research besides the near-death experience. They are:

NDA	nearing-death awareness[14]
ADC	after-death communications[15]
PBE	prebirth experience[16]

As research continues to become more sophisticated, the idea of a life continuum is no longer relegated to the dustbin of sloppy interviews or dismissed as wish fulfillment. We are coming of age as we advance into the third millennium, and we are seeing ourselves through a broader and more exacting lens. What we are discovering is what we've previously overlooked—that other dimensions of life, other realities, have always existed. We just didn't have the right tools before to properly identify them.

NINE

ALIEN EXISTENCES

Architects of the future are being brought onto your
planet from their home civilizations. They asked to
come, and come they will. They each have a mission.

Tauri, of the Ogatta Group

Besides the phenomenon of missing twins, we have the
enigma of missing fetuses. This mystery occurs when women
find themselves pregnant without having had sexual contact
with a man and then suddenly are not pregnant weeks or
months later. This is termed the "missing fetus syndrome."[1]
Seldom is there verification of these reports—a fact that does
nothing to quell tales of "space nappings," of aliens swoop-
ing down to reclaim "half human/half alien" babies that will
finish developing and be raised aboard their spaceships (note
the similarity to claims about some missing twins). The purpose of these "hybrids," a few women have been told via
mental telepathy, is to seed a new race of beings.

Investigations into these strange pregnancies, as well as of
extraterrestrial contacts and UFO abductions, involve millions of people worldwide. Gone is the day when the subject of alien existences could be tossed off as fodder for bad
dreams or creepy fiction. Currently, enough evidence exists
to put the subject on the table for legitimate discussion.
Since human genetics, fertility, and children are now con-

sidered central to the entire alien issue, and because so many kids report varied types of contacts with such beings, we are obliged to talk about it too.

I first began tracking otherworldly contacts in the sixties. Then as now, I noticed that experiences involving aliens often ran in families. It was the five children of nurse-turned-psychic Pamela Williams of Mason, Michigan, for instance, who caused her to think twice about the reality of extraterrestrial visitors, particularly when her son Leonard was four. "I got up in the night to check on the boys in their upstairs room," remembered Pamela, "and to my surprise Len was sitting on the floor looking out the window. I asked what he was doing out of bed. 'I've been talking to the star people.' He then pointed out the window and I saw a bright light in the night sky. 'What are they saying to you?' I asked. 'They're telling me that is my home.' [When he got] a little older he began seeing UFOs almost daily, and being a typical boy, thought it was fun to upset his father by pointing them out." David, her youngest son, was even more emphatic. "Before he was eighteen months old, he would greet and talk to beings I could not see. He had dramatic dreams very young, science-fiction dreams of other planets, other races, spaceships, etc. He was always waking me up in the night to tell me about them."

A successful psychotherapist (who prefers to remain nameless) confided to me similar memories from her own childhood: "I was said to have walked and talked very early, but to have been adultlike and solemn. At four or five I remember standing in our backyard looking at the southern sky, and thinking—'That is my home. My real mother and father left me here and when I've suffered enough they'll come back and get me.' Throughout the years I had waves of what I called homesicknesses: an overwhelming longing that came and went periodically no matter where I was and had nothing to do with my earth family or where we lived."

While researching the near-death phenomenon, I routinely encountered child experiencers who would say things like, "I feel like an alien" or "a misfit" or "a foreigner." And they'd admit to being *homesick* for what they had to leave behind in order to come to earth. As compelling as these stories are, and there are many of them, I question whether the claims made by kids really signify extraterrestrial origination, or if, maybe, something else is involved.

Numbers from my research reveal:

Adult Near-Death Experiencers
(based on 3,000 interviews)

Identified with being from another planet	20%
Claimed to have been abducted by a UFO	9%

Child Near-Death Experiencers
(based on 277 interviews)

Identified with being from another planet	9%
Identified with being from another dimension	39%
Claimed to have been abducted by a UFO	14%

Not as many adult experiencers said they had been abducted by a UFO as did child experiencers, although a few of them noted that they occasionally dreamed of seeing spaceships. The most surprising difference I found between adults and children concerned "place of origin." Adult near-death survivors who remembered either during or right after their episodes that they had come to this planet from another one numbered 20 percent, a figure dwarfed by the percentage of youngsters who recalled not so much other planets as multidimensional realms. No adult I interviewed ever expressed his or her origin in terms of multi-dimensionality; only kids did this.

Before we explore this unusual variance, it would be helpful to first gain a sense of how child experiencers express themselves on the subject of alien existences.

Larrick Stapleton, Wynnewood, Pennsylvania. NDE at age four, tonsillectomy. "I was raised in a traditional southern Midwest, WASP household, was confirmed as a Presbyterian in a somewhat fundamentalist church, and did extremely well in school and with all matters academic. I saw colors and lights as a small child and have always heard 'music,' and was the subject (victim) of some form of abduction experience when I was just an infant. Like most matters out of the ordinary, none of this was ever discussed and it was in fact denied."

Robin H. Johnson, Plymouth, New Hampshire. NDE at age two, drowning. "The same spiritual being who I envisioned when I drowned later appeared before me and two other women, this time in a prearranged conscious state. After both encounters with this being, I was visited by extraterrestrials. Unlike other abductees, I love my abductors and miss them when they leave."

P. Bradley Carey, Burlington, Washington. NDE at age thirteen, choked by another child. "My first alien encounter was at the age of ten. My father realized that he had left his wallet at the lake, but he didn't want to go back alone, so I went along. We were about three-quarters of the way there, in a very isolated area, when the lone streetlight went out, and the lights and car engine suddenly stopped. My father shifted the car into park and was about to turn the key, when we both saw a strange glowing ball in the sky above and to the front of us. We watched this ball until it disappeared between the hills. [In] what seemed only moments later, the streetlight was suddenly on, as were the car lights and engine. Never once did my father touch the key, so there is no way he could have restarted the car. Without saying anything to each other, we continued on our way, found the wallet, and headed back home. Once we arrived, we discovered that the entire trip took nearly three hours longer than it should have."

Diego Leon Valencia Lopez, Bogotá, Colombia. NDE at birth, during emergency surgery; several more NDEs in adulthood. His wife, Dina, is the translator. "When Diego was five years old, a member of his family died. He walked to a cornfield on the family ranch while waiting for the adults who had gathered. There he saw a kind of robotic figure surrounded by a luminous brilliance. Telepathically the figure called to Diego. It seemed to him that the being picked up something, then the light disappeared, and Diego remembers having floated.

"When [Diego] had chicken pox, his room in a very big old house was in the corridor and had no windows. Suddenly, there was a yellow glow in the middle of the room that made him immensely happy. His brother also saw the light before it disappeared.

"At the age of seven, [Diego] went with his brother to the farm and saw a bright light. They both lost four hours and don't remember what happened.

"At nine, he left school at 11:00 A.M. with a friend. Diego sat on the footwalk and gazed below at lots of fruit and vegetable trees. Among very high weeds he saw two beings with

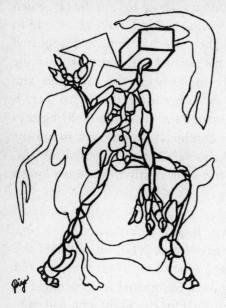

Stylized creation made by Diego Lopez to depict his emotional response to the actual visitations he says he has witnessed.

casks. One of them inclined toward the other and had a kind of strainer. Diego could see them clearly, yet suddenly and instantaneously, he found himself in a very different place without having walked there, and was very tired. When he finally made it to his friend's house for lunch, he discovered that he was two and a half hours late and his friend had already left for school.

Again that same year, he was hiding in thick bushes with his brother. Unexpectedly, he saw a splendorous light from which a voice spoke to him. His brother fell asleep in the grass, and Diego was lifted up. He flew to a faraway place. He remembers saying good-bye, and then [he] returned to find his brother still sleeping. This splendorous light being appeared many times after that, with a special murmur [Diego] learned to distinguish."

Dina Ledvua

Portrait of Diego sketched
by his wife, Dina, while
he was meditating.

*Francis Piekarski, New Martinsville, West Virginia. NDE at age
five, drowning; at twelve from high fever and bone infection.* "I feel
called to warn the world of impending danger. Chernobyl
was an example come true. Shortly, I feel that the world will
be in turmoil. UFOs will play a big part in the transition.
The Blessed Mother (Marian devotions) will play an equally
large part. I personally feel I must help after the disasters to
start a new lifestyle. We have formed a group here to investigate psychic revelations and alien contacts."

*Joe Ann Van Gelder, Newport, Vermont. Nine NDEs as a child,
varied causes.* "I had a past-life regression to inquire into a
recurring dream I'd had over the years. In this regression, the
dream was experienced as a partial memory of a time when
I'd come from Venus to help those on Mu [a "lost continent" in the Pacific]. When the [regression] facilitator told

me to 'Go home to Venus,' my reply was, 'I'll go to Venus, but it's not home.' She then instructed me to 'Go home,' and my consciousness 'flew.' I left this galaxy far behind. When the sense of movement stopped, my consciousness was suspended far out in the Universe in what I described as 'the plasma between the planets and the stars.' When the facilitator asked me for a description, I 'saw' that I was one of a small group of Sparks of Light. When she asked me what I was doing, my consciousness merged with the Spark that was me, and I experienced it consciously. I told her, 'I'm not *doing* anything; I'm *being* . . . waiting to be sent out again.' "

Renditions of alien existences from child experiencers rarely match adult accounts. Children, for the most part, are seldom impressed with the idea of extraterrestrials or spinning spheres. For them, coming from Venus, Mars, Sirius, or the sun is not so much an indicator of "home," as Joe Ann Van Gelder made clear, as it is recognition of a way station. Most regard the special lights they see as guides who accompany them through stages of learning as their soul progresses along God's Eternal Spiral of Remembrance. It is teen and adult experiencers who are excited by the proposition that they are the aliens and that they came to earth from another world, or that they were abducted and taken aboard a spaceship and that they now have an ongoing relationship with aliens—even though little ones ages three to five actually report more of this than do experiencers who are older.

Children, especially the very young, strongly relate to something else entirely . . . *life in other dimensions of existence.* Two distinctive expressions of this awareness were evident to me back in the sixties; this same pattern emerged again in my near-death research, and I have encountered it regard-

less of country or culture throughout the millennial generation. Because this pattern of multidimensionality is so per-
vasive, it behooves us to take a deeper look.

There are two distinctive expressions of multidimensionality.

ORIENTATION TO THE LIFE CONTINUUM People with this
orientation are concerned with life embodiments and the
progression of souls. Their memories embrace prebirth and
after-death realms as exit and entrance points to a single
lifestream or life continuum inhabited by the type of spirit
they once were and will be again—their true home. (The
majority—about three-quarters of the total—recall this.)

ORIENTATION TO THE COSMOS People with this orientation
are concerned with the universe's inner workings and the
progression of Creation. They identify with formlessness:
gases, attractors, particle sparks, waves, energy pulses, plasma,
and so forth, as if the substance of their being and their place
of residence were one and the same—part of the mechanism and structure that hold together and maintain Creation
itself. (Fewer respondents—about one-quarter—claim this
orientation.)

In the following sections I interpret these two types of
multidimensional awarenesses.

ORIENTATION TO THE LIFE CONTINUUM

The first three paragraphs of *The Famished Road,* by Ben
Okri,[2] are the best example I can offer of what this orien-

tation seems to be like for youngsters and how they tend to reminisce from this perspective:

> In the beginning there was a river. The river became a road and the road branched out to the whole world. And because the road was once a river it was always hungry.
>
> In that land of beginnings spirits mingled with the unborn. We could assume numerous forms. Many of us were birds. We knew no boundaries. There was much feasting, playing, and sorrowing. We feasted much because of the beautiful terrors of eternity. We played much because we were free. And we sorrowed much because there were always those amongst us who had just returned from the world of the Living. They had returned inconsolable for all the love they had left behind, all the suffering they hadn't redeemed, all that they hadn't understood, and for all that they had barely begun to learn before they were drawn back to the land of origins.
>
> There was not one amongst us who looked forward to being born. We disliked the rigours of existence, the unfulfilled longings, the enshrined injustices of the world, the labyrinths of love, the ignorance of parents, the fact of dying, and the amazing indifference of the Living in the midst of the simple beauties of the universe. We feared the heartlessness of human beings, all of whom are born blind, few of whom ever learn to see.

A multidimensional child oriented to the life continuum is similar to other child experiencers, except that he or she has a unique focus or sense of self as spirit and as a resident of the realms of spirit. These children know from their earliest years that their existence on earth is temporary and for the purpose of fulfilling the progression of the soul, their own and others'. Because "home" is the luminous lifestream they came from and will return to, many of them speak objectively about past lives and incarnations in life-forms one might consider alien. A higher level of spirituality and truth is more important to them than parental preferences. As a result, they are open to and highly tolerant of diverse viewpoints. Attempts to make them fit society's mold are usually a waste of time. Service occupations and philanthropic endeavors interest them.

ORIENTATION TO THE COSMOS

Youngsters who identify themselves this abstractly seem to be possessed of almost pure intellect. They spout advanced concepts about things like waveforms, energy sources, and power grids in the same manner in which the average child might quote football scores. And they are explicit about their origins: "Not here, not there—elsewhere." Just because these children occasionally mention other planets does not mean they consider themselves to be from them. To make such an assumption completely misses the scope of their panoramic worldview. "Home," for them, is the universe at large.

Multidimensional/cosmos children are unlike those who remember going back and forth through the life continuum, although most are knowledgeable about soul progression. These kids act as if they have never been on this or any other planet before, and, frankly, they consider the human body a useless, clumsy appendage. They seem utterly unconcerned with family issues or personal relationships. What matters to them is saving the earth and making repairs, which means they are drawn to vocations in fields such as ecological sustainability (the "green" movement), alternative power sources, leading-edge science, large-scale economic and medical reforms, and photonics.

These children present us with an entirely new slant on the way "life" is defined. For them, each aspect of Creation has its own aliveness and consciousness; for instance, they insist that the very gases we breathe are living intelligences. Often they refer to themselves as stewards, guardians, or "keepers" of that which enables cells and molecules to exist, rather than as evolving spirits. Although their memories could be interpreted as awareness in the womb (plasma, waves), these youngsters are insistent on being here for "the changes," and insistent that the universe they refer to is the larger one, the cosmos. Most state they were "called" here by a signal the earth sent out for help, *not* by their parents' desires.

I have observed that multidimensional/cosmos children in general:

> *Live in their own head* to the extent that it's almost as if nothing else exists from their neck down. As a result, they tend to have body-coordination problems. Exercise and massage can alleviate this and help them connect with their bodies. Tai chi, aikido, and mind-stretching games generally appeal more to them than sports like football or wrestling.
>
> *Are either unusually slow or fast* to speak, walk, and learn basic tasks. They do not respond to injury, pain, or illness as other children do, since they dissociate easily. It often may seem as if they're "not all there," when in fact they are actively engaged. These children readily "see"

the soul level of a person; hence, they tend to know the truth of a given situation before those around them, and are not easily fooled.

Are not social by nature, nor are they distracted by sexuality, except to ponder why distinct genders exist. Large crowds bother them.

Are ultrasensitive to pollution emissions, heavy ozone levels, loud sounds/music, intense sunlight, temperature and pressure variations, unpleasant vibrations and odors.

Do not understand death, nor the fact that they could lose their body if they don't take care of it. Often they don't even relate to primary survival needs. Role-playing games help them identify with human selfhood and show them how to thrive and enjoy life on the earth-plane. Experiential hands-on projects enable them to appreciate the solidity of matter and its purposefulness.

Are very loving but emotionally "removed." Caring for pets, creating gardens, and doing volunteer work are the kinds of activities that allow these children to experience the give-and-take of relationships while learning about emotions and the myriad ways to express them.

The key to successfully raising multidimensional/cosmos children, at least so far as I have seen, is to arrange opportunities whereby they can relate one object to another, one feeling to the next, each action to its consequence. Once they catch on to the basic maneuvering of physical matter and human behavior—and it may take them longer than the average child to figure this out—they more than make up for lost time in their rapid-fire manner of absorbing information.

Two examples of this unusual type of child are the Cabobianco brothers, Flavio and Marcos, of Buenos Aires,

Argentina. Underpinning their story is what their parents, Alba and Nestor, both Freudian psychologists, went through in trying to understand them. Raising their unusual sons opened up vast spiritual realities unexplainable using Freud's limited analytical techniques. So, Alba and Nestor switched to the field of transpersonal psychology and were instrumental in introducing this new field to psychology professionals in Argentina, at a time when the totalitarian government there still squelched independent thought. That they were successful is amazing in itself.

Alba had a near-death experience as an adult after succumbing to toxic gases. She feels that her episode prepared her for the sons she would have, by opening her consciousness to otherworldly realms and greater truths. Through correspondence translated by Alejandra Warden, a close friend of the Cabobianco family, Alba revealed that she kept a journal of her sons' prescient disclosures, and noted the age at which each boy provided another glimpse into their multidimensional/cosmos world. While still quite young, Flavio began to write and called himself a "cosmic messenger," here to speak about spiritual things. "Now that this world is starting to be less physical, other children like me are going to come," he presaged. "Human beings are different now. They are going to be more open. I am here to calm people who are frightened by the changing energy of Earth. But I am also here to help the guardian souls, the nonphysical beings who are involved in the changes." According to Flavio, the guardian souls keep the systems of creation going. They maintain the different levels of universal integrity. He feels that his job as a communicator is to be a bridge that reaches in both directions—to humans about the truth of spiritual worlds, and to the guardian souls about how people on earth are adjusting to planetary change.

At eight years of age, Flavio Cabobianco met Ama, a woman interested in the notes his mother took, in his drawings, and in the little books he made. She edited the material and was instrumental in writing out his explanations of the diagrams he and his brother, Marcos, made of the universe. As a book took shape, Ama suggested the order of the chapters and that family comments be included. Before Flavio was a teenager, *Vengo del Sol (I Come from the Sun)* was published in Argentina and became a best-seller.[3] "When I wrote *I Come from the Sun,* I was very young and I knew few words," Flavio admitted. "I want to make clear that it isn't the physical sun I'm talking about, but the spiritual sun."

Vengo del Sol is the most astonishing book written by a child that I have ever seen. The drawings, and Marcos's and Flavio's explanations of them, bespeak a consciousness far wiser than that of most adults; the tower diagram, which shows how all of creation evolves and was done when Flavio was seven (Marcos helped), is nothing short of spectacular.

When I met the brothers (thanks to Alejandra Warden we were able to engage in spirited dialogue), I was struck by what I had recognized decades before: there seems to be a class of people who incarnate on earth who have detailed memories of having existed as bits and pieces of Creation before hearing a call for help and agreeing to take on density of form so the call could be answered. It's almost as if *the universe is capable of using parts of itself to save itself.*

I know this idea is far-fetched, but consider a paper published in a recent edition of the *Frontier Perspectives* at Temple University in Philadelphia, Pennsylvania. In "Is Dead Matter Aware of Its Environment?"[4] the author, Peter Graneau, dissects physics and comes to the conclusion that either an outside agency controls universal gravitation, or *particles of matter have knowledge of each other.* Children have been telling me for decades what Graneau arrives at through physics: *the universe is alive!*

There have been "bridges between worlds" such as Marcos and Flavio Cabobianco throughout history, but now there are more of them. Their bodies seem to have a different density than those of "regular" people; they are extraordinarily sensitive, especially to touch and to food; and many find it imperative to wear nonallergenic clothing. Living around others or being in a crowd can be difficult for them, as they have no armor from previous incarnations to help them handle negativity.

Certainly there are child experiencers of near-death states who report interactions with extraterrestrials and speak of worlds and races unlike those associated with earth. Spaceships fascinate them and the abduction drama becomes an almost routine part of their daily lives. These youngsters, however, are in the minority.

Of intrigue to our discussion of alien existences, though, is the book *The Omega Project: Near-Death Experiences, UFO Encounters, and Mind at Large,* by Kenneth Ring.[5] A retired psychology professor who has spent over twenty years (a few more than I) researching near-death states, he has come to recognize similarities between people who experience abduction incidents and those who have near-death episodes.

Ring posits the existence of an "encounter-prone personality" found in people who have distinctive, spiritually sensitive, and visionary psyches that may, collectively, represent the next stage in human evolution. He found that many of the people who report extraordinary encounters had childhoods marked by various patterns of trauma, stress, and/or child abuse. "They're more likely to dissociate from ordinary reality and then tune in to other realities where they can feel safe," he explained. And these other realities, or "imaginal realms," as Ring calls them, are not to be confused with fantasy worlds. "Imaginal realities have a matrix or structure to them, and you can tune in to them if you have the right faculty of perception. If you are already sensitized to these imaginal realms, then your imagination, acting like an organ of perception in its own right, can simply detect these realities. When you talk to people who have had NDEs, they say things that imply that this is a hyperreality. Things like, 'This experience was more real to me than life itself is real.' Here's an analogy: We cannot see the stars when the sun shines, but when sunlight is absent the starry heavens are revealed. But, obviously, the stars have been there all along." Ring continues: "I think these people may possibly be—one word I could use is *edglings*. They may be closer to a higher development of human potential than most of us. What happened to them is exactly the same thing that happens to a person being trained to be a shaman in a tribal society . . . [they] develop a kind of spiritual sensitivity and a sense of the sacredness of Earth."

Ring's work relies heavily on child abuse issues to underscore his theory of encounter-prone personalities. I did not find this same degree of cause/effect relationship in my own research, even though some of my cases do fit his model. His ideas about the existence of imaginal realms and the sensitivity that can be achieved to access them does correspond with what I have seen. Having a near-death experience, regardless of how it is caused, is sufficient to sensitize an individual to multiple dimensions of reality. The link is *not* child abuse, but a brain shift/spirit shift. Many children are now born this way. It is a characteristic of what may be a new race emerging in our midst.

Unlike in previous years, recent newspaper headlines have forever changed how we regard the notion of life in outer space. One scientific finding after another has heralded: "Mars was once warm and moist, and may have supported life." "Discovery boosts odds for life on Jupiter moon." "Black holes, neutron stars make space swirl like water." "Hubble telescope snaps picture of undetected giant in Milky Way." "Massive pillars in Eagle nebula harbor a stellar nursery." "Evidence of anti-gravity force found." "Particle found to have mass." "Extra–solar system planet photographed."

The arrogance of thinking we are the only life-form in our universe is weakened not only by science, but by some of our astronauts, who are breaking their code of silence about UFO-type craft accompanying their space flights. Some of their revelations were printed in the newsletter *Woodrew Update.*

Greta Woodrew, LL.D., and her husband, Dick Smolowe, LL.D., for seventeen years published the *Woodrew Update,* a newsletter devoted to the exploration of alien contacts, health issues, and ecological responsibility.[6] Both are businesspeople with sterling credentials whose lives were turned upside-down when Greta was first contacted by Tauri, an extraterrestrial who said she was from the "Ogatta Group." In *Woodrew Update* volume 17, number 3, Greta and Dick quoted statements made by American astronauts, among them Gordon Cooper: "For many years I have lived with a secret, in a secrecy imposed on all specialists in astronautics. I can now reveal that every day, in the U.S.A., our radar instruments capture objects of form and composition unknown to us. And there are thousands of witness reports and documents to prove this, but nobody wants to make them public." And from Scott Carpenter: "At no time, when the astronauts were in space, were they alone: there was a constant surveillance by UFOs."

I have no doubt that extraterrestrials exist in some form and that they are capable of making contact with human beings. Physical evidence is too great, sightings too numerous and confirmed by too many people, to be tossed aside as group hypnosis or self-deception. But neither am I convinced of the extent to which this phenomenon is organically composed. Imaginal worlds, as defined by Kenneth Ring, are much more powerful in their effects on experiencers who visit them and in their utter realness than most of us can appreciate. And imaginal worlds are multidimensional in appearance and are associated with the life continuum in the sense of being like layers of luminous fabric enfolded throughout coherent worlds of structured form. People can be taught how to access these realms; some have a natural talent to do so, or accidentally find themselves there because of a sudden occurrence like a near-death state or a shamanistic vision quest. (Shamanistic-type consciousness is often initiated by some sort of near-death-like ritual or mind-altering drug, which is not to say that such states can be sustained for any period without considerable training.)

Once an individual's perception is opened to the "bright worlds," that individual is never quite the same again.

When traveling "behind the veil" we may find ourselves on an alien planet, or in the life continuum, or as part of the plasma that fills the so-called vacuum of outer space, depending upon which layer or matrix we have accessed. During our visit, we may experience our selfhood in ways that would be considered extraordinary in human terms.

Tom Repasky of Portland, Oregon, describes such a trip, labeling himself a "walk-in."

Tom fell off a cliff ledge when he was fourteen years old, and bounced for twelve feet after striking rocks. Although he does not remember a near-death episode, he does display the full range of aftereffects, including an extremely high IQ. He is employed today as an expert in the computer industry, is married, and has a daughter. According to Tom: "About twelve days after the accident, I (the current occupant) found myself wandering about space. I was aware of my awareness and was able to examine my history. This history was many years long (thirty-five thousand years). During that time I had been only an observer of life and the planet earth. I felt a strong desire to experience life as a human and began my journey into a human form. The result of this journey was my entering the form I now animate, [which] is called Tom. I began life within a 14-year-old body without any personal body memories. My first action was to cause the form to move and in doing so, I surprised the hospital staff, who said I had been in a coma. Of course, these words were just noise to me, and it was not until several weeks later that I began to understand and imitate human speech."

Ruth Montgomery, in her book *Strangers Among Us,*[7] coined the term "walk-in" to accommodate situations in which one soul could exchange places in a given body with another one; in other words, the resident or birth soul could "walk out" or leave for whatever reason, and a new one could "walk in." Ostensibly, this exchange would take place during periods of unconsciousness or as a result of a near-death experience. In Montgomery's view, the two souls must agree to the exchange or it couldn't occur, and the incoming soul was obligated to fulfill the duties of the birth soul before new goals could be initiated. Today, the term "walk-in" has become in some circles a generic catchall to explain away the aftereffects of a brain shift/spirit shift as evidenced by a transformation of consciousness. Curiously, *all* of the various indicators of a "soul exchange" that are generally cited by proponents of the walk-in theory *exactly* correspond to aspects of a typical near-death scenario and the aftereffects that follow. So far, the brain shift/spirit shift model has held up to rigorous scrutiny; the walk-in theory hasn't.

Tom Repasky's experience matches the criteria for a walk-in as currently espoused by an organization called Walk-ins for Evolution (WE) International,[8] with one important distinction. Tom remembers being without form during a thirty-five-thousand-year history as an aware intelligence. As he tells it, "There wasn't one [soul] to replace another." Tom's description of his former existence echoes the multidimensional/cosmos child's explanation of the formlessness with which he or she identifies. Could brain damage account for his inability to embrace selfhood in a personal manner? Perhaps, but this ready explanation does not address why his superior intelligence and cascade of aftereffects can be traced directly to his accident. I suspect that Tom is brain shifted, *not* brain damaged, and multidimensionally oriented to the cosmos rather than a "walk-in."

Tom, like ever so many of the child experiencers quoted in this book, bears all the marks of a new vanguard of children who have been entering the earthplane in large numbers since the sixties, and especially since 1982. These children regard themselves and the lives they lead quite differently than have their elders, and in terms that bespeak a more quixotic viewpoint. They are tolerant of ambiguity, capable of parallel-thought processing, unusually creative, and at home with a complexity of lifestyles that would seem foreign to the generations before them. And with each decade that passes, their creative and intuitive intelligence soars. They are tomorrow's children, today.

TEN

A NEW RACE ABORNING

Evolutionary quantum leaps occur when a species is
faced with possible extinction. Now, at such a threshold,
we are discovering the neurological methods that medicine people and visionaries have mastered so elegantly
and have used to make quantum leaps into the future.
These capabilities of our brains, once awakened, allow us
to enter a transtemporal reality where we can hear the
voices of the ancient ones in the wind, heal our planet,
and summon our destiny.

Alberto Volloldo

The signs are evident, all of them, that a new race is emerging in the midst of us *right now!*

Child experiencers of near-death states present us with
the best possible model we can use to recognize this
birthing. And the millennial generation, children born from
1982 to 2003, as named by William Strauss and Neil Howe
in their seminal achievement *Generations,*[1] are "marked" in
the sense that already many of them are displaying characteristics typical of the psychological and physiological
changes that occur after the brain shift/spirit shift engendered by the near-death phenomenon.

Youngsters are being flung into this shift quite literally by the millions worldwide, and a whole generation is being born this way, as if they were somehow preprogrammed. One does not have to be a scientist or a psychic to know that something astonishingly spectacular is rising from the "knife's edge" of birth and death . . . a new force awakens.

All cultures that have ever existed (and that can be traced) have had legends and stories that describe major evolutionary leaps in consciousness and in genetic structure that have occurred and will yet occur in the human family. The purpose of these leaps, it is said, is to quicken and refine our species in a vast process of growth that will advance humankind from hardly more than a probability at the dawn of time (or, some say, as mere drones engineered for slave labor by an elitist class bent on mining the earth's gold for their home planet),[2] to the highest and best achievement level and frequency of vibration possible for us to attain in a quest to become more intelligent and god-like. And each such advancement, we are further instructed to know, is visibly marked—the people differ afterward and their differences show.

Since these ancient legends and stories *exactly* portray our current situation, a synopsis of their message is in order. Visionary truth is just as important as scientific findings. We need both to give us perspective.

Various traditions of esoteric knowledge (loosely referred to as "mystery school teachings") mention the altering of the lifestream whereby new "waves" or "rays" or "worlds" can arise. Earlier in this century, the famous seer Edgar Cayce[3] called these time frames "the coming forth of root races." He did not mean "race" in the context of genetic subgroups, but used the term "root races" to indicate species-wide, evolutionary mutations. He targeted 1998 to

2010 as the years when the next "advancement" would be recognized.

Other, older teachings predicted that a total of seven root races would appear, each one fulfilling its potential, before the human species reached ascendancy. The first four races were essentially described as soul, amorphous thought forms, physical thought forms, and human beings. What was presaged for our current period is the emergence of the fifth root race,[4] those who have quickened in spiritual awareness and genetic makeup. This collection of visionary knowledge holds that two more root races will emerge before the development of "Hu-man" ("God-man") is over. The Christian Bible has in essence the same message— that we are gods in the making and that we are ever growing in spirit. An example of this message is Psalm 82:6: "I have said, ye are gods; and all of you are children of the most high."

By using the colors of the rainbow to depict the energy levels of vibrational frequencies, it is possible to combine esoteric teachings, be they from psychics, mystics, prophets, or visionaries, into one comprehensive chart. This chart focuses on the soul's evolution through human form via the stages of a mind awakening to its greater potential.

Esoteric Teachings of Soul Evolution Through the Awakening of the Human Mind

Levels of Energy	States of Awareness	Types of Consciousness
Red	Physical	Physical: the earthplane; survival issues and individual power
Orange	Astral	Astral: invisible "blueprints"; inner guidance and heightened sensitivity

Continued

Levels of Energy	States of Awareness	Types of Consciousness
Yellow	Mental Concrete	Mental: the intellect; decision making and personal will
Green	Mental Abstract	Buddhic: awakening to spirit; initial enlightenment and enlarged worldview
Blue	Higher Intuition	Atmic: self as individual; enlightened knowing and wisdom
Indigo	Inspiration	Monadic: fully individuated; the indivisible whole
Violet	Spiritual	Divine: aligned with soul power; surrender to God's Will

If we take the concept of root races (for example, soul, amorphous thought forms, physical thought forms, human beings, and those quickened in spiritual awareness and genetic makeup, as well as two more higher forms of embodiment yet to come), and insert each type into the chart beginning at the top, we arrive at a broad picture of what may indeed be the evolutionary destiny of humankind—a growth progression referred to in esoteric traditions transculturally. According to the diagram, the fifth root race, which is aborning now, comes under the purview of the blue vibration.

And the "blue race" has specifically been mentioned in some prophesies as the quantum leap that would evolve from within the midst of the human family during the final years of the Piscean age. Supposedly, this "fifth race" would be as unlike its predecessors as crystal is unlike clay. Zodiacal cycles, or ages, are approximately 2,160 years long. After the third millennium begins, and by the year 2,020, we will enter the long-awaited age of Aquarius, presumably a time when the rigors of science will join with the wisdom of inner knowing to produce societies dedicated to the economics of shared projects and international achievement, rather than to the wanton violence and enslavement of dictatorships.

The members of the blue race, as the architects of the Aquarian age, are said to be exceptionally aware, highly developed both intuitively and intellectually, and comfortable with ambiguity and complex challenges, thus made to order for the demands of the twenty-first century. Visionary traditions also refer to differences in their biological structure—unusual digestive systems and allergies, differences in eyesight, heightened faculties, a noticeable sensitivity to foods, light, sound, and energy fields, plus an amazing ability to function with the least amount of stress during difficult situations.

Descriptions of the blue race are resonant with the typical aftereffect characteristics of the average child experiencer of near-death states, as well as with what pediatricians worldwide are reporting about the newest crop of infants.

A contemporary voice on the subject of the new race aborning in our time is Gordon-Michael Scallion. He is known as an intuitive futurist and modern-day prophet, and is probably most famous for his "future maps" of North America, as well as his predictions of global earth changes. It was he who several years ago affirmed that the fifth root race is the blue race and linked it with the then soon-to-appear blue star, which he later identified as the comet Hale-Bopp. He associated the manifestation of both of these developments with Christian beliefs about the Second Coming of Christ, and also with the Native American prophecy of the White Buffalo and the portentous 1994 birth, in Janesville, Wisconsin, of an all-white female buffalo calf, since identified by tribal elders and medicine men as the fulfillment of their prophecy and the signal that the New Age has begun.[5]

In his book *Notes from the Cosmos: A Futurist's Insights into the World of Dream Prophecy and Intuition,*[6] Scallion discusses at length the blue star and the blue race. He states: "According to NASA astrophysicist Michael Mumma, Comet Hale-Bopp is the largest comet ever, bright as an evening star. It has an elliptical orbit of about four thousand two hundred years, which intersects the plane of our solar system at key times. I believe the last time an intersection occurred was two thousand years ago, about the time of the Wise Men's journey to Bethlehem. I believe with all my heart and soul that we are once again experiencing the Messenger Star, whose task it is to signal the beginning of our next spiritual awakening and the millennium of peace. I will make a new prediction here regarding this subject. I believe that between 1998 and 2001, everyone with eyes to see and ears to hear will experience a spiritual event that parallels the event that occurred two thousand years ago. How will this awakening occur? Will a spiritual leader bring the message, or will it be a collective experience? I believe both will occur."

Of the blue race, he says: "All children born after '98 shall be telepathic at birth and many born prior shall exhibit such abilities. The physical body shall change to reflect the vibrational changes of Earth under the influence of the Blue Star. . . . All races of people shall have a bluish tint to the skin as a result." Scallion also predicts changes in the makeup of the human eye and the way the new race will see, and claims that communication will be possible between these new humans and the animal and spiritual worlds.

By the age of two, Scallion says, many will have mastered multiple languages; by three or four, they'll be aware of their most recent past life. Blue race humans will also have a much longer lifespan, upward of about two hundred years, according to Scallion, and they will put service to others above personal gratification.

If Gordon-Michael Scallion is correct in his contention that the blue star governs the soul, then blue race people will be more spiritually inclined than their mothers and fathers. One such person of bluish skin has already made an impact in her native land of India and in other countries where she has traveled. As word of her existence and her powerful spiritual teachings spread, her influence is fast becoming global. Her name is Mata Amritanandamayi, and her story is both a tear-jerker, because of the abuse she received as a child, and an inspiration, because she turned her own nightmare into a miracle, enabling her to help transform the lives of thousands.

Mata Amritanandamayi: A Biography, written by one of her devotees, Swami Amritasvarupananda,[7] tells of a poverty-stricken mother who had a wonderful dream about giving birth to Lord Krishna (one of the most popular of the Hindu deities). The next morning, without a single clue that she might be about to deliver a real baby, she intuitively realized she must prepare to do just that. With hardly enough time to spread out a mat and lie down, she gave birth to a daughter. But this was no ordinary daughter. Not only were the entire pregnancy and birth pain free, but the infant was born smiling and without a cry; she lay in the lotus posture of hatha yoga, her fingers in the position symbolizing oneness of the individual self with the Supreme—and she had dark blue skin! The parents were panic-stricken and feared that the baby's strange complexion might be a symptom of disease, the peculiar posture she assumed at birth perhaps a sign of abnormal bone structure. Medical exams detected no abnormalities, nor was there anything in the family's genetic line to account for this. The baby they named Sudhamani was an anomaly.

As stated by Swami: "Eventually, over the course of time, this dark-blue changed into black. Yet, when the little girl's desire to behold the vision of Lord Krishna intensified, her skin colour once again assumed its blue hue. Even today, especially during the Divine Moods of Krishna and Devi, one can observe this dark blue skin tone. Ironically, it was due to this blue-black hue that in the future, Damayanthi [Sudhamani's mother] and other family members would look upon the child with great disdain. This aversion for the dark child would eventually become the cause of her becoming the downtrodden servant of the family and relatives.

"From the moment of the tiny girl's birth, the family began noticing unusual signs which would only be understood years later. . . . One day, after turning six months old, the little girl suddenly stood up and straight-away walked across the verandah. Soon after this, she started running which filled everyone's heart with wonder and joy. Unlike most other children her age, Sudhamani started speaking her mother tongue Malayalam when she was barely six months old. Her passion to sing the Divine Names manifested as soon as she began to speak fairly well. At the tender age of two, without instruction from anybody, she began saying prayers and singing short songs in praise of Sri Krishna."

As a toddler, Sudhamani established a daily habit of melodiously chanting the Divine Names aloud, a practice that continues to this day, and she would sing with devotional fervor compositions she created to honor Lord Krishna. By the time she was five, her spiritual activities had become extraordinary. In school she evidenced a brilliant intellect and memory that so threatened her parents that they pulled her out of her classes, assigning to her instead an ever-increasing load of chores. This only served to intensify her ecstatic devotional moods. Yet the more spiritual she became, the more determined her family was in heaping hard work and physical abuse upon her, convincing themselves that she must be insane. That Sudhamani survived her childhood is a miracle in itself. She forgave all her tormentors, noting that they had committed their crimes in ignorance. All later became her students once she was recognized as a teacher and servant of God. Today she is referred to as the Mother of Immortal Bliss.

Although having blue skin is not necessarily a condition of blue race "membership," Mata Amritanandamayi has exhibited all the traits of a brain shift/spirit shift since her birth in 1953. Her exceptional devotion to God and knowledge of a higher, more spiritual order of life mark her as one of those "blue ones" of the fifth root race.

The human race *is* adapting, mutating, altering, transforming. We are becoming something else.

As *Homo habilis* we were hardly more than fossils.

As *Homo erectus* we were active, social, and inventive.

As *Homo sapiens* we were highly organized thinkers and clever builders.

As *Homo sapiens sapiens* we went to the moon and computerized society.

John White, who has written extensively in the fields of consciousness research and human development,[8] classified our fifth species advancement as *Homo noeticus.* This species will have the ability to access the higher mind. Declares White: "There will never be a better world until there are better people in it, and our potential for growth to higher consciousness is what enables us to 'build better people,' beginning with ourselves."

I would be exaggerating here if I claimed that all those born into the millennial generation are fifth root race types. What percentage will actually represent evolution's quantum leap, or, perhaps, signal a devolution into children incapable of caring or compassion, no one really knows. Today's headlines are crammed with ample stories of both extremes. Still, it is possible to project ahead to surmise about what I am certain will be the majority of our new citizens—the fourteenth generation of the United States. Few are better qualified for such a task than historical demographers William Strauss and Neil Howe and the respected astrological researcher E. Alan Meece.

Strauss and Howe remark that, even now, the larger number of these youngsters are proving to be unusually civic minded, optimistic, collegial, competent, possessed of a powerful type of energy, and collective in purpose, expecting praise and rewards while generously passing on the same to others. And they save more money than they spend on conveniences. "The Millennials show every sign of being a generation of trends—toward improved education and health care, strengthening families, more adult affection and protection, and a rising sense that youths need a national mission."[9]

E. Alan Meece, in his tour de force of astrological patterns in history *Horoscope for the New Millennium,*[10] further delineates what might be expected from the millennials by dividing them into four categories according to year of birth. The early wave, born from 1982 to 1983, he calls an exuberant yet mellow group, like children of the seventies, often lacking in discipline and focus, yet definitely explorers who like to live on the edge. Those born from 1984 to 1988 he terms "benevolent entrepreneurs" who, unlike the first group, are ambitious and disciplined, rather conservative, but with a sense of great duty to society and humankind. He notes that a very precocious bunch with outstanding potential checked in between 1988 and 1995. But he warns that while they possess great talents and leadership skills, they could also be cold, calculating, and one-sided in their assessment of how the world should be changed. The final group, born from 1996 to 2003, he claims will be "flame throwers" with exceptionally outgoing, irrepressible, freedom-loving, rebellious natures—reformers quick to challenge authority.

Make no mistake, youngsters born before and during the millennium's turn are already and will continue to be as demanding as they are curious, and *they are powerfully obsessed with a need to change things.* Although many of them come across as all heart, at least initially, that seeming compassion can readily devolve into senseless acts—as already evidenced by kids who have killed other kids in Littleton, Colorado; Pearl, Mississippi; Jonesboro, Arkansas; Edinboro, Pennsylvania; and Springfield, Oregon. As Strauss and Howe pointed out, the millennial generation *must have a national mission,* clear goals to aim for, and teachers unafraid of their unusual abilities, or the awesome promise they carry within them could be misdirected or squandered.

One woman keenly aware of the millennials' collective drive and how to direct it is Linda Redford of Santa Monica, California. An adult experiencer of a dramatic near-death episode, she was given instructions while "dead" on how to create a learning program for today's children that would enable them to address their personal concerns, while disciplining their minds and restoring a sense of honor and value to their world. Named The Adawee Teachings

(*Adawee* is Cherokee for "guardians of wisdom"), the learning program has already been tested in a number of schools. One teacher said, "I have never experienced such unity in a classroom [as I have] since this pilot project ended." The program, written in collaboration with Redford's daughter Anne Vorburger, consists of course studies, a self-discovery book, and a T-shirt each student receives that says, *"I am important to the world. The world is important to me."*[11]

"My vision, instead of healing the damage from childhood, is to stop the damage from happening in the first place," Redford explained. Just tallying up the faxes and messages on her Web site from children participating in The Adawee Teachings, and from teachers clamoring for more information on how to continue the program, proves that her guidance to do this was right on. With Redford's permission, I have included the honor code from The Adawee Teachings.

The Honor Code

Principles for Planetary Citizenship. For each principle, the adult version is presented first, followed by the child's perspective.

HUMILITY

I am aware that I can learn from all that was created.
I can learn from the sky, a clock, a tree, my friends, and my mom and dad.

RESPONSIBILITY

I am aware that my words and actions are powerful and have a positive or negative impact on my life, as well as on others and the environment.
When someone is sad I can sit quietly and talk with them until their sadness leaves, or I can tease them and make them sadder.

RESPECT

I am aware that all that was created has purpose and value.
I'm learning that even a tree has a living spirit that I need to honor.

HONESTY

I am aware that being truthful takes courage and is easier when I
 am open to my feelings.
When I'm truthful with others they learn to trust me.

GENEROSITY

I am aware that sharing my abundance creates harmony and balance.
When I share with others, I feel good inside.

FORGIVENESS

I am aware that mistakes can be opportunities for growth and
 understanding.
*When I say I'm sorry I understand that I have hurt you, and when I
 hurt you I hurt myself.*

WISDOM

I am aware that there is an intuitive knowing within me that can
 guide me to make wise choices.
*I am learning that inside me I have a wise part that knows what's
 best.*

All children crave knowledge and hunger to learn. All children know that each thing is alive and can communicate. All
children often flow into mind states that heighten knowing.
All children are as much aware of spirit realms as of the earthplane. All children like to test their perceptions for usefulness.
All children are emissaries of divine love and forgiveness.

A child's reality is the basis of a child's truth.

Deny the reality, and you deny the child.

ELEVEN

THE PROMISE

The true doctrine of omnipresence is that God reappears with all his parts in every moss and cobweb. The value of the universe contrives to throw itself into every point. If the good is there, so is the evil; if the affinity, so the repulsion; if the force, so the limitation. Thus is the universe alive.

Ralph Waldo Emerson

Mainstream society tends to marginalize creative intuitives. Individuals interested in consciousness transformations, those who have been through one (such as experiencers of near-death states), along with others of like mind, have for years been busily networking with each other to counteract mainstream bias and create a subculture of their own within society. Their preferences as a group include:

Community-based economies and regional trade;
Revitalized main streets, amateur theater, and open workspaces;
Small-scale, sustainable developments with Internet sales capacity;
Appreciating the uniqueness of place and history, the importance of neighborhoods;
Individual knowingness and intuition in health and healing;

Handmade objects over mechanical or plastic ones;

Homes that fit into natural landscapes, herbal gardens;

Recycling, remodeling, and restoration;

Pilgrimages to sacred and holy places, respect for the feminine;

Commitment to lifelong growth and learning and the exchange of ideas;

Loving, committed relationships, a sense of global as well as national citizenship;

Public service, volunteerism, civic responsibility;

Spiritual development, the personal experience of awakening to spirit realms and communicating with Source.

Thanks to early prototypes of the fifth root race, the steady groundswell toward a definable subculture that is more holistic in attitude has exceeded expectations and is now recognized as a force to be reckoned with by opinion pollsters.

Sociologist Paul Ray, vice president of the San Francisco–based market research firm American Lives, Inc., labels this growing faction as cultural creatives,[1] and he estimates that forty-four million Americans, or roughly one-fourth of the population, fit this category. He considers them a kind of integral culture that merges modernism with traditionalism, East with West, to create a Renaissance mindset. Ray warns that cultural creatives are almost angry in their demand for authenticity, an observation underscored by Charlene Spretnak in her book *The Resurgence of the Real: Body, Nature, and Place in a Hypermodern World.*[2]

At the current rate at which cultural creatives are becoming politically active, and to the degree to which fifth root race newcomers continue to identify with them and support their agendas, the tipping point, or change threshold, may soon be reached. Tipping points are endemic to history, always unpredictable as to exact timing, but ever fateful in collapsing that which has grown inefficient, top-heavy, or "out of touch" with the citizenry (e.g., the dismantling of the Berlin Wall and every dictatorship that has ever existed). There comes a time when sheer numbers are enough to trigger a massive shift in the prevailing order. (Sometimes other tyrannies arise, but the original one does not and cannot last.)

Societies everywhere are now in this position, vulnerable to a tipping point. Computerization has made it possible for any individual to coparticipate in dissolving borders and outmaneuvering governments. A sense that moral integrity and social justice should matter more than global power relations and religious fundamentalism is gaining majority strength. Nothing less than *the evolution of society itself* is at hand; the subculture is poised to become the dominant culture.

The twenty-first century will bear witness to the driving force of this "third wave," which is neither left nor right, liberal nor conservative, traditionalist nor modernist, but an integrated stream of consciousness that is intolerant of business as usual; it is more reformist than revolutionary.

And, *as this third wave moves into the third millennium, "thirdway" principles will emerge as the way to live and do business.*

I devoted an entire chapter in both *Future Memory* and *Solstice Shift: Magical Blend's Synergistic Guide to the Coming Age*[3] to a discussion of third-way principles. Here is a summary of what I have discovered about the Third Way.

I have noticed that when faced with life issues, we tend to react in one of three ways: (1) we play ostrich and pretend the situation away; (2) we label it an enemy or a devil and attack; or (3) we confront the situation squarely and honestly, search for the truth behind the appearance, and take decisive steps to initiate a constructive solution. The first way creates victims, the second victors (conquerors), and the third responsive and responsible participants in life, committed to growth and learning.

This third way of dealing with life issues is the way we transcend duality, get beyond victors and victims, good and evil, darkness and light. The Third Way requires mediation and diplomacy skills, mindful attention, and a willingness to consider *what is appropriate* as a greater priority than self-centered interests. It takes time to learn and patience to initiate, and it necessitates cooperation and compromise, but it is the only modality that holds any promise for a worthwhile future. The Third Way upholds dignity and authenticity and wholeness, and wholeness is spirituality made manifest.

When we live in accordance with the Third Way, we decrease tension. While a certain amount of tension is necessary to existence, too much tension depletes initiative and restricts growth. The fulcrum of Third Way balance is *forgiveness,* as forgiveness releases tension and promotes patience. When we resist forgiveness, the resulting tension keeps us from transcending. We need to let go to grow. We need to forgive.

Another individual who has written extensively on third-way principles is Walter Starcke, a former Hollywood luminary who underwent a spiritual transformation many years ago and has since become a devoted student of the Christian Bible and a mystic. In his new book, *It's All God,*[4] he reveals that the Third Way (ascension consciousness) is *reconciliation.*

But he cautions: "As long as we believe that we must constantly and only think beautiful, subjectively satisfying thoughts, we are creating the very duality we claim to deny. What I am saying is, we can reconcile the objective level [materiality] without denying its subjective nature [spirituality] only if we simultaneously see both its infinite oneness and its limited form. By doing this, we close the gap and experience the only true absolute: All inclusiveness."

Reconciliation and inclusiveness are the keys to understanding what fuels millennial generation attitudes and the cultural creatives as a subculture. For them, elitist thinking has lost the fashionable appeal it once had.

The "age of globality" arrived in 1998. With it came the realities of photonics (enhanced fiber optics for the information superhighway); interspecies communication (apes trained via sign language to converse with humans); biochemistry "marking" (medication engineered to meet the needs of each person as an individual); natural-systems agriculture (high-yielding perennial grains grown together to cut waste and weeds); weather pattern study (links between weather effects and sex repression, warfare, and social violence);[5] cloning issues (life-science companies dominating seed and DNA sequence patents).[6]

The third millennium is quickly becoming a science-fiction world made fact.

Curiously, the vast majority of children rescued from death's finality by advanced technology have near-death experiences that prepare them for . . . advanced technology.

These kids aren't coming back as the dutiful fulfillments of their parents' dreams so much as, in their own quiet way, the mountain movers of the twenty-first century. And don't breathe a sigh of relief that at last we have a generation of children who are courteous and civic minded. *These young-sters are instilled with a sense of mission, and they are powerfully obsessed with a need to change things. This is their promise and their destiny.* And they will insist upon the spirit-led worship and uncommon lifestyles that arise from having a personal relationship with God.

They are "imagineers," creative problem solvers rewired and reconfigured to make significant contributions to a society desperately in need of fresh new ideas. But it will take innovative and courageous adults to point the way.

The exceptional legacy of retired teacher Muriel Freifeld of Potomac, Maryland, gives us such a model. She experienced a near-death episode while stuck in the birth canal that infused her with a lifelong mission to educate children in ways that would empower them. She suffered frequent parental and sibling abuse as a youngster, but what hurt her the most was her inability to communicate her visions and her inner knowing. She was branded "stupid" and became suicidal. Her extremely high IQ wasn't recognized in time to prevent her rebelliousness, low grades, and school truancy. She "knew" her subjects but fumbled over the technicalities of how to format what she knew (the same situation faced by Bill of Atlanta, in chapter 3).

Once Muriel was an adult, she began the college track, did well in math, showed an unusual sensitivity to music, won many prizes in art, and excelled in the double major of psychology and early childhood development. Her career as an innovative teacher and later as founder of New Visions for Child Care, Inc.,[7] a project endorsed by the governor of Maryland, is exemplary. And, of her three children, two have become pioneering physicians in new surgical techniques and treatment of infectious diseases, and the other is a well-known southern artist. Muriel's life is an example of what can happen when the potential enhanced by a brain shift/spirit shift is unleashed, to the benefit of the many.

According to my research statistics, child experiencers of near-death states, like Muriel Freifeld, are showing us how to have long-lasting, healthy relationships and marriages; how to excel in work and succeed in spite of the stress from downsizing and layoffs; how to live simply, yet more enjoyably; how to have a meaningful, satisfying, and active life. Those who seemed socially retarded during their earliest years have proved that the learning reversals and faculty and intelligence enhancements that may have seemed burdensome when they were children and young adults can indeed be integrated, and in ways bordering on the miraculous. Some of the participants in my study, for example, are now doing advanced DNA research, working on new healing tools for surgeons, producing significant patents and inventions, establishing compassionate birthing and dying centers, and creating new measures to recycle waste materials, protect the environment, and build better homes for less cost. Not all are college graduates. They don't have to be. Even as amateur scientists and social visionaries, their achievements already have astounded and amazed us, and will continue to do so.

It is true that child experiencers do not process brain shifts/spirit shifts in the same manner as do adult experiencers, and their episodes are likely to impact them in more powerful ways—as the cases discussed in this book illustrate. Aftereffects tend to overwhelm, because the context in which they must be integrated has yet to be established in the lives of the children who must grapple with them. A simple chart puts this situation in perspective.

Effects of a Transformation of Consciousness (Brain Shift/Spirit Shift)

Adults	renewal	new life	a growth event—"course correction"
Children	rebirth	new race	an evolutionary event—"species advancement"

To transform the world, people must transform . . . and they are.

Those who were thrust into this transformational shift via the near-death phenomenon may be so changed that even before-and-after photographs may bear little resemblance to each other, to say nothing of attitudes, personalities, and body functions; their lives are often turned upside down. But even those who have been touched by the Holy Spirit during church services, people who have gone on shamanic vision quests, or those who have devoted themselves to lives of service and prayer may exhibit the same aftereffects, the same shift.

While near-death states might be Creation's way of selecting helpers who might not otherwise volunteer, transformations by choice enable one to be more in control of any trauma or confusion the aftereffects may foster. In other words, 'tis better to go willingly than to be shoved, for the spiritual will not forever be denied.

The brain shift/spirit shift that happens in such large numbers to today's youngsters offers the most compelling evidence yet that mind itself, that collective "reservoir" of intelligence, is also evolving. It is possible, for instance, to take the four types of near-death experiences discussed in chapter 3 and reconsider them in this manner.

- *Initial Experience:* an introduction for the individual to other ways of perceiving reality; stimulus.
- *Unpleasant or Hell-like Experience:* a confrontation with distortions in one's own attitudes and beliefs; healing.
- *Pleasant or Heaven-like Experience:* a realization of how important life is and how every effort that one makes counts; validation.
- *Transcendent Experience:* an encounter with oneness and the collective whole of humankind; enlightenment.

Rather than looking at these as four *types* of near-death experience, we might more appropriately recognize in them four *stages* of awakening consciousness. These stages of awakening begin with the first stirring of something greater, an initial awareness; then move to confrontation with the bias of perception, followed by opportunities to cleanse and start anew; then to the bliss and the ecstasy of self-validation and the discovery of life's worth; until, at last, the moment comes when unlimited realms of truth and wisdom are unveiled.

Since consciousness appears to have the capacity to grow, change, and evolve, individually *and en masse,* one implication is the existence of thought fields that all of us must be capable of drawing from and adding to automatically or at will. This idea has been postulated scientifically and is currently being tested at the urging of Rupert Sheldrake, best known for his breakthrough theory of "morphic resonance" (the existence of universal thought fields), detailed in his book *A New Science of Life: The Hypothesis of Formative Causation.*[8]

The fact that so many children experience near-death episodes indicates to me that the mechanism for stimulating a brain shift/spirit shift may be part of our "equipment" as human beings—our *birthright*—nature's assurance that, as individuals and as a species, we will continuously readjust as evolution readies itself for major advancements.

After decades of research and sessions with thousands of people, I am convinced that once we understand the import of *brain shifts* (which are visible and can be clinically tested and measured), and *spirit shifts* (which are invisible and signify the movement of spirit forces and the development of true faith) . . . we will solve the secret of how the human family and mind itself evolve and for what purpose.

I can make this extravagant statement because my work has shown me that *brain shifts/spirit shifts are the engine that drives evolution and thus the destiny of humankind.*

Experiencers of this dual shift have described the "light" that they encountered in terms that suggest there may be *three very different types of light* that exist beyond those we are consciously aware of and beyond the light known in the realms of earth life.

The Three Types of Subjective Light

Type	Color	Function
Primary Light	Colorless	A pulsating presence or luminosity usually perceived as frighteningly awesome, a piercing power, raw essence; the origin of all origins
Dark Light	Pure black yet often with velvety tinges of dark purple	A shimmering peaceful depth usually perceived as "The Darkness That Knows," a source of strength and knowing, sanctuary; the womb of Creation
Bright Light	The range of yellow-gold-white	A brilliant radiance usually perceived as an almost blinding glow that emanates unconditional love, a warm inviting intelligence, union; the activity of Truth

These three lights are consistently referred to, regardless of person, age, or background, as more real than the manifest light on earth and more powerful than any source humankind could harness—including the sun's rays and "zero-point" energy (the "stuff" of the universe; untapped electromagnetic energy).

These lights seem to reveal aspects of Creation in a manner that implies that they may represent the outworking of Divine Order. There is no human connotation given to their function by most experiencers (such as black as negative/evil or white as positive/good), but, rather, an identification is made with the handiwork of God.

The main effects I have observed in the people who claimed to have experienced them were: from Primary Light, deep mystical knowings and more radical changes in a sense of reality and life's purpose; from Dark Light, gentle reassurances of being nurtured and supported while linked to larger evolutionary processes; from Bright Light, displays of a broad range of visibly heightened abilities and sensitivities as if the physical body was transmuting.

It is my belief from what I have seen that the "light" and light imagery of near-death and other transformative and enlightening states are but the reflection of a power surge as it registers upon or imprints the consciousness of the one who experiences it. What is perceived as light may well be a "power punch," varying by degrees of charge. To dub transformative episodes as mere "light experiences" misses the rich complexity of their true nature.

Individuals who return to earthplane awareness after such an event almost immediately gain a sense of future. Irrespective of the other aftereffects and whether that sense of future can signal higher brain development and the emergence of the higher mind, the futuristic revelations that pour forth from experiencers can be taken literally. Referring especially to child experiencers, their apocalyptic visions differ somewhat from those of adult experiencers.

Kids seem only moderately concerned with the earth changes numerous prognosticators and prophets have targeted for the years between 1998 and 2007. Even the fabled date of May 5, 2000, when all the planets in our solar system, as well as our moon, align in a single tangent that could put tremendous pressure on the earth's crust, leaves them with a wry smile and a simple shrug of the shoulders. But jump ahead to a time when they could be parents or even grandparents, and their composure abruptly changes. "That's what I came back for," they say, "to help the earth and prepare the people. I am here for *the changes.*"

This message of theirs sounds similar to that of adults, until the math is calculated as to how old each child would have to be to match the description they give of themselves during that cryptic time. Regardless of the child's age when interviewed, *the same period emerges—between 2013 and 2029.*

This same timespan was highlighted by Strauss and Howe in their study of repetitious cycles in American history. To understand the significance of this period, they ask that we recall the parallel eras of the Glorious Revolution, the American Revolution, the Civil War, the Great Depression, and World War II. "How will this crisis end?" they wonder. They then offer this comment: "Three of the four antecedents ended in triumph, the fourth (the Civil War) in a mixture of moral fatigue, vast human tragedy, and a weak and vengeful sense of victory. We can foresee a full range of possible outcomes, from stirring achievement to apocalyptic tragedy."

Of interest is the fact that on December 21, 2012, the Mayan calendar ends—one year before the "darkening skies" of the crisis projected by Strauss and Howe. The

Mayans believed that time as it currently is experienced will end when their calendar does. Strauss and Howe, although hopeful about the future, admit that all indicators do indeed predict this period as one of unusual importance, and in all probability global in its repercussions.

Yet the ending of the Mayan calendar does *not* signify an end to history, just to time as we know it, for their calculations were based on sun cycles of approximately twenty-six thousand years each. What ends in 2012 is the span of the Fourth Sun. The Fifth Sun begins immediately after, with the fifth root race at the ready to handle the possible acceleration of time and energy as the earth passes into a region of highly charged particles called the photon belt. Slated to last for two thousand years, this photon immersion elicits curiosity from scientists who remain unconvinced of its supposed effects, if any, and awe from the more mystical who see in this event a period when both sixth and seventh root races can emerge to complete the ascendancy of human evolution on this planet. We will have to wait either way to see if the photon belt is a fizzle or a true phenomenon. Regardless of how things turn out, the years 2013 to 2029 can't help but be momentous as we enter a new timespan—that of the Fifth Sun.

Right now, however, an extraordinary credo begs for attention—the integration of science and religion, the reconnection of the head with the heart. And this affects near-death research, as well.

Ken Wilber, who almost single-handedly launched the transpersonal revolution in psychology several decades ago with the publication of his first book, *The Spectrum of Consciousness*,[9] granted a rare interview with Mark Matousek that was carried in the July/August 1998 issue of *Utne Reader*.[10] In the article, Wilber confirmed that the relation-

source Section

eb site orders: $10.00 (U.S.); several options for pay-
ment. If you don't have a computer, try your local
library.

il orders: $15.00 (U.S.) plus $3.00 shipping and handling
n the United States, $4.50 in Canada, and $9.00 in
ther countries. Personal checks or money orders. Send
o: You Can Change Your Life, P.O. Box 7691,
Charlottesville, VA 22906-7691.

hen you visit the Web site, look up how to obtain the
Shift/Spirit Shift Model, and be certain to check out
Marketplace of NDE-Related Items of Interest, a trea-
trove of offerings from a host of near-death experi-
rs or those like them. Marketplace is a public service
with videos, music, art, and all types of inspired products and services that could make a difference in your life.
ucts and services are posted free of charge. The
ketplace exists nowhere else. Take advantage of it!

ship between science and religion is the most critical issue
facing society, a rift that he believes is tearing the planet
apart. "When you take into account that 90 percent of the
world's population has a religious outlook based on some
kind of mythology—God the Father and so on—and that
the standard scientific view gives these myths as much credibility as they give the tooth fairy . . . you see the problem
clearly. There's an enormous split between reason and
meaning that must be healed."

Wilber builds a compelling case stating that prerational
"messages" and "channeling" are all too often little more
than New Age silliness when compared to the mystical, esoteric core undergirding all of the world's great religions—a
truth based on direct experience *that was thoroughly tested*
before it was offered to adherents as a reproducible experience. States Wilber, "Science has managed to reproduce itself
for two to three hundred years, while mystical science has
been doing it for at least two to three thousand years. This is
not insignificant." In *The Marriage of Sense and Soul,*[11] his
newest work, he describes how art, ethics, and science can be
integrated *without* compromising their important differences.

Pierre Teilhard de Chardin[12] has been my inspiration
because of how he managed to combine the intellectual
with spirituality. Even in consideration of the numinous
power I experienced in death, it has been the twenty-plus
years I spent tempering revelation with careful fieldwork
and analysis that showed me the real wonder of life's pulse.
My discovery was Teilhard de Chardin's—research *is* the
highest form of adoration—for me a marriage of science
and spirituality as Wilber described.

I offer this book as the next chapter in our mutual quest
for knowledge and understanding. I offer this final story as
the next step in the desire we all have for wisdom.

A friend of mine and fellow near-death survivor participated in some of the most gruesome and horrific battles of the Vietnam War. He was also part of the army contingent that was the first to arrive after the massacre of Vietnamese civilians by U.S. troops at My Lai in 1968. Picking his way through the carnage, he happened upon a little girl digging a grave to bury her family. The task was hers, since she was the only family member left. My friend spoke with the child and she told him she must now do as her father had once asked of her: *look for the light on the dark side of the mountain.* "I will make a garden over the graves of my family and plant food," she explained, "so people going by will never go hungry."

The "wisdom of angels" is in our children, for they *know* what is true . . . thus is the promise of childhood, now, and always.

WEB SITE OF
P.M.H. ATWATER,

www.cinemind.com/atwa

My Web site exists as a cyberlibrary of m
death research, the spiritual approach to l
use of intuitive abilities. Changes are n
time, especially to my travel schedule.

Space limitations in this book negated
appendixes that were to appear as back
readers to know that these missing appe
over the Web site for immediate downlo
directly as printed text. The 125-page te

Tips for the "Child" in All of Us
  Tips on Counseling and Therapy
  Tips on Education, Music, and the
  Tips on Being in Spirit
  Tips on Coping with Spirit
  Tips on Soulmaking

Research Methodology
  Includes the questionnaire form use
  riencers in this study

ship between science and religion is the most critical issue facing society, a rift that he believes is tearing the planet apart. "When you take into account that 90 percent of the world's population has a religious outlook based on some kind of mythology—God the Father and so on—and that the standard scientific view gives these myths as much credibility as they give the tooth fairy . . . you see the problem clearly. There's an enormous split between reason and meaning that must be healed."

Wilber builds a compelling case stating that prerational "messages" and "channeling" are all too often little more than New Age silliness when compared to the mystical, esoteric core undergirding all of the world's great religions—a truth based on direct experience *that was thoroughly tested* before it was offered to adherents as a reproducible experience. States Wilber, "Science has managed to reproduce itself for two to three hundred years, while mystical science has been doing it for at least two to three thousand years. This is not insignificant." In *The Marriage of Sense and Soul,*[11] his newest work, he describes how art, ethics, and science can be integrated *without* compromising their important differences.

Pierre Teilhard de Chardin[12] has been my inspiration because of how he managed to combine the intellectual with spirituality. Even in consideration of the numinous power I experienced in death, it has been the twenty-plus years I spent tempering revelation with careful fieldwork and analysis that showed me the real wonder of life's pulse. My discovery was Teilhard de Chardin's—research *is* the highest form of adoration—for me a marriage of science and spirituality as Wilber described.

I offer this book as the next chapter in our mutual quest for knowledge and understanding. I offer this final story as the next step in the desire we all have for wisdom.

A friend of mine and fellow near-death survivor participated in some of the most gruesome and horrific battles of
the Vietnam War. He was also part of the army contingent
that was the first to arrive after the massacre of Vietnamese
civilians by U.S. troops at My Lai in 1968. Picking his way
through the carnage, he happened upon a little girl digging
a grave to bury her family. The task was hers, since she was
the only family member left. My friend spoke with the child
and she told him she must now do as her father had once
asked of her: *look for the light on the dark side of the mountain.*
"I will make a garden over the graves of my family and plant
food," she explained, "so people going by will never go
hungry."

The "wisdom of angels" is in our children, for they *know*
what is true . . . thus is the promise of childhood, now, and
always.

WEB SITE OF
P.M.H. ATWATER, LH.D.

www.cinemind.com/atwater

My Web site exists as a cyberlibrary of my work with near-death research, the spiritual approach to life, and the positive use of intuitive abilities. Changes are made from time to time, especially to my travel schedule.

Space limitations in this book negated including the three appendixes that were to appear as back matter. I want my readers to know that these missing appendixes are available over the Web site for immediate downloading, or from me directly as printed text. The 125-page text contains:

Tips for the "Child" in All of Us
    Tips on Counseling and Therapy
    Tips on Education, Music, and the Arts
    Tips on Being in Spirit
    Tips on Coping with Spirit
    Tips on Soulmaking

Research Methodology
    Includes the questionnaire form used with child experiencers in this study

Resource Section

Web site orders: $10.00 (U.S.); several options for payment. If you don't have a computer, try your local library.

Mail orders: $15.00 (U.S.) *plus* $3.00 shipping and handling in the United States, $4.50 in Canada, and $9.00 in other countries. Personal checks or money orders. Send to: You Can Change Your Life, P.O. Box 7691, Charlottesville, VA 22906-7691.

When you visit the Web site, look up how to obtain the Brain Shift/Spirit Shift Model, and be certain to check out the Marketplace of NDE-Related Items of Interest, a treasure trove of offerings from a host of near-death experiencers or those like them. Marketplace is a public service filled with videos, music, art, and all types of inspired products and services that could make a difference in your life. Products and services are posted free of charge. The Marketplace exists nowhere else. Take advantage of it!

WEB SITE OF INTERNATIONAL ASSOCIATION FOR NEAR-DEATH STUDIES (IANDS)

www.iands.org

IANDS exists to impart knowledge concerning near-death experiences and their implications, to encourage and support research dealing with the experience and related phenomena, and to aid people in starting local groups to explore the subject. They have numerous publications, among them the scholarly *Journal of Near-Death Studies,* a general-interest newsletter, *Vital Signs,* and various brochures and materials. Membership in this nonprofit organization is open to anyone; dues are annual and include various benefits.

Donations to cover operating expenses are always needed and always welcome, especially for the NDE Research Fund. Audiocassette tapes of IANDS conference speakers are available. Ask for their list of national and international chapters (Friends of IANDS), should you be interested in visiting any of them. Individual reports about near-death episodes are solicited for the archives; to make a report you will need to fill out a form, so please ask for one.

Memberships, back issues of their publications, and conference tapes can now be ordered directly from their Web site.

Check out their section on actual experiencer episodes; it is growing as more and more people are willing to share their stories. Do start an IANDS group in your area if there isn't one already; invite members from the group Compassionate Friends to come, as those who have lost a child find great comfort when exposed to near-death experiencers and materials. The 1999 IANDS Conference was held in Vancouver, British Columbia. In 2000 it will be held in Philadelphia, Pennsylvania.

International Association for Near-Death Studies
P.O. Box 502
East Windsor Hill, CT 06028-0502
phone (860) 644-5216
fax (860) 644-5759

NOTES

Do not wait for leaders; do it alone, person to person.

Mother Teresa

Preface

1. P. M. H. Atwater, *Coming Back to Life: The After-Effects of the Near-Death Experience* (New York: Dodd, Mead & Co., 1988; Ballantine Books, 1989).
2. P. M. H. Atwater, Lh.D., *Future Memory: How Those Who "See the Future" Shed New Light on the Workings of the Human Mind* (New York: Birch Lane Press, 1996; Charlottesville, Va.: Hampton Roads Publishing Co., 1999).

One: Evolution's Nod

1. William Strauss and Neil Howe, *Generations: The History of America's Future, 1584 to 2069* (New York: William Morrow, 1991). This is the best reference I have found for identifying the distinctive agendas each generation brings to the fore, and addressing the historical context of the years in which they lived.
2. Sharon Begley, "The IQ Puzzle," *Newsweek,* May 6, 1996, 70–72.
3. Melvin Morse, M.D., with Paul Perry, *Closer to the Light: Learning from the Near-Death Experiences of Children* (New York: Villard Books, 1990).
4. "Is There Life After Death?" *U.S. News & World Report,* March 31, 1997, 58–64.
5. Michael Cremo and Richard Thompson, *Forbidden Archaeology:*

The Hidden History of the Human Race (Alachua, Fla.: Govardhan Hill, 1993).

6. Richard Milton, *Shattering the Myths of Darwinism* (Rochester, Vt.: Park Street Press, 1998).

7. Michael J. Behe, Ph.D., *Darwin's Black Box: The Biochemical Challenge to Evolution* (New York: Free Press, 1996).

Two: Brain Shift/Spirit Shift

1. P. M. H. Atwater, Lh.D., *Phase II—Brain Shift/Spirit Shift: A Theoretical Model Using Research on Near-Death States to Explore the Transformation of Consciousness.* Available as a sixty-four-page, single-spaced cyberbook research report on my Web site: www.cinemind.com/atwater (various options for payment). Or as a bound book from You Can Change Your Life, P.O. Box 7691, Charlottesville, VA, 22906-7691. Query for costs, or access Web site.

2. *New Scientist* magazine (January 8, 1994) cited the latest findings of Nicholas Humphrey, a senior research fellow at Cambridge University, who discovered that emotions are primary. His work concerns "sensory consciousness," a term he coined for the brain's role in feeling. Other researchers have joined in, each adding more information about the importance of emotion and how it influences the mind. A good book on this subject is Antonio R. Damasio's *Descartes' Error: Emotion, Reason, and the Human Brain* (New York: Grosset/Putnam, 1994).

3. Marianne Frostig and Phyllis Maslow, "Neuropsychological Contributions to Education," *Journal of Learning Disabilities* 12, no. 8 (October 1979): 538–552. Also refer to the book *Evolution's End,* by Joseph Chilton Pearce (San Francisco: Harper San Francisco, 1992).

4. Glen Rein is a senior researcher at the Institute of Heart Math, and can be reached through them at 14700 West Park Avenue, Boulder Creek, CA 95006; (408) 338-8700.

5. Refer to Richard E. Cytowic, M.D., *The Man Who Tasted Shapes: A Bizarre Medical Mystery Offers Revolutionary Insights*

into Emotions, Reasoning, and Consciousness (New York: Tarcher/Putnam, 1993).

6. Howard Gardner, *Creating Minds* (New York: Basic Books, 1993). Howard Gardner, a psychologist and codirector of the Harvard Project on Human Potential, profiled great minds of the twentieth century in an attempt to characterize genius. He discovered: that discarding accepted ideas of what is possible can make it easier to take new ideas seriously; that connecting the unconnected leads to insight; and that a tolerance for ambiguity is crucial to creativity. He points out that the word "intelligence" means "to select among," indicating the importance of detail recognition. But genius *shakes together* or *clusters* information, much as a child would, to arrive at different or larger concepts.

7. Refer to Anna Wise, *High Performance Mind* (New York: Putnam, 1995). The brain normally operates at varying brainwave speeds. Wise created audiocassettes of music and sound frequencies so that anyone who wanted to could have an opportunity to achieve simultaneous "awakened" mind states. These tapes are available from: Kit Walker, Tools for Exploration, 47 Paul Drive, San Rafael, CA 94903; (800) 456-9887.

8. Refer to the article "Brain Waves Move Computer Cursors," *The New York Times,* March 7, 1995.

9. Cited in note 2 of the preface.

10. Ibid.

11. Todd Murphy, "The Structure and Function of Near-Death Experiences: An Algorithmic Hypothesis." This paper is currently being updated, as research is ongoing, but contact the author for a copy of what he has completed thus far. Write to him at P.O. Box 170414, San Francisco, CA 94117. The editor at *Journal of Near-Death Studies* has expressed an interest in publishing this paper when it is completed. Murphy's paper "Recreating Near-Death Experiences: A Cognitive Approach," was published in *Journal of Near-Death Studies* 17, no. 4 (Summer 1999). His groundbreaking research of child experiencers in

Thailand is due for publication in *Journal of Near-Death Studies* 18, no. 2 (Winter 1999).

12. Arnold J. Mandell, "Toward a Psychobiology of Transcendence: God in the Brain," in Richard and Julian Davidson, eds., *The Psychobiology of Consciousness* (New York: Plenum Press, 1980).

13. Michael A. Persinger, Ph.D., *Neuropsychological Bases of God Beliefs* (Westport, Conn.: Praeger, 1987).

14. Wilder Penfield, M.D., *The Mystery of the Mind* (Princeton, N.J.: Princeton University Press, 1977).

15. Raymond A. Moody, Jr., M.D., with Paul Perry, *Reunions: Visionary Encounters with Departed Loved Ones* (New York: Villard Books, 1993). Moody is the one who coined the term "near-death experience" and launched the entire field with his first book, *Life After Life*.

16. P. M. H. Atwater, Lh.D., *Beyond the Light: What Isn't Being Said About the Near-Death Experience* (New York: Birch Lane Press, 1994). The title was altered in the paperback edition to *Beyond the Light: The Mysteries and Revelations of Near-Death Experiences* (New York: Avon Books, 1995).

17. For more information about the imagery in otherworld journeys, peruse the following: Joseph Campbell, with Bill Moyers, *The Power of Myth* (New York: Doubleday, 1988). Ioan Couliano, *Out of This World: Otherworld Journeys from Gilgamesh to Albert Einstein* (Boston: Shambhala, 1991). Manley P. Hall, *The Secret Teachings of All Ages* (Los Angeles: Philosophical Research Society, 1978). Richard Heinberg, *Memories and Visions of Paradise: Exploring the Universal Myth of a Lost Golden Age* (Los Angeles: Tarcher, 1989). Carl G. Jung, *Man and His Symbols* (New York: Laureleaf, 1997).

18. For an enlightening discourse on this force, refer to Adolf Holl, *The Left Hand of God: A Biography of the Holy Spirit* (New York: Doubleday, 1998).

19. James Hillman, *The Soul's Code: Character, Calling and Fate* (New York: Random House, 1996).

20. David Spangler, *The Call* (New York: Riverhead Books, 1996).

21. Larry Dossey, M.D., *Prayer Is Good Medicine* (New York:

HarperCollins, 1996). Also, Larry Dossey, M.D., *Healing Words: The Power of Prayer and the Practice of Medicine* (New York: HarperCollins, 1997).

22. Kathleen Norris, *The Cloister Walk* (New York: Riverhead Books, 1996). Also, Kathleen Norris, *Amazing Grace* (New York: Riverhead Books, 1998). The quote I used came from *Amazing Grace*. I find the title of her latest work intriguing, because many researchers attach the notion of "amazing grace" to the near-death phenomenon, and Norris herself behaves and writes as if she once had such an experience.

23. Ken Wilber, *A Brief History of Everything* (Boston: Shambhala, 1996).

24. Kathleen J. Forti's *The Door to the Secret City* is available both as a book and as an audiocassette dramatization. Contact: Kids Want Answers, Too!, 1544 Bay Point Drive, Virginia Beach, VA 23454.

25. To obtain a copy of Henry Reed's paper "Intimacy and Psi: Explorations in Psychic Closeness," or to be notified of his workshops and speaking schedule, write to: Henry Reed, Ph.D., c/o A.R.E., P.O. Box 595, Virginia Beach, VA 23451.

Three: A New View of Near-Death States

1. Raymond A. Moody, Jr., M.D., *Life After Life* (Covington, Ga.: Mockingbird Books, 1975).

2. Kenneth Ring, Ph.D., *Life at Death* (New York: Coward, McCann & Geoghegan, 1980).

3. International Association for Near-Death Studies (IANDS), P.O. Box 502, East Windsor Hill, CT 06028-0502; (860) 644-5216; fax (860) 644-5759; Web site www.iands.org. Ask for brochure "Active Support Groups." Also, refer to pages 237–238 for more information about the IANDS Web site.

4. Howard Gardner, *Frames of Mind* (New York: Basic Books, 1983). An excellent review of this book appeared in *Utne Reader,* September/October 1990, 82–83. It was written by Thomas Armstrong of *Mothering* magazine.

5. Linda Kreger Silverman, Ph.D., and her assistant, Betty

Maxwell, can be reached through the Institute for the Study of Advanced Development, 1452 Marion Street, Denver, CO 80218; (303) 837-8378. Silverman's work in the field of gifted children is extensive and well documented. I would encourage anyone interested to investigate her offerings.

6. To obtain Silverman's monograph on Dabrowski, ask for a copy of "The Moral Sensitivity of Gifted Children and the Evolution of Society" when you contact her. Also request her rendition of Dabrowski's theory, which discusses his ideas about positive disintegration of psychological structures in favor of compassion, integrity, and altruism. Refer to note 5 for address and phone number.

Five: The Impact of Aftereffects

1. Marlene Spencer, M.Ed., "Dissociation: Normal or Abormal?" *Journal of Near-Death Studies* 14, no. 3 (Spring 1996): 145–157.

2. Compassion in Action: The Twilight Brigade is spreading nationally and internationally. Inspired by the conviction of near-death survivor Dannion Brinkley that no one need die alone, the organization works with volunteers to serve in hospices, hospitals, and home care to provide a loving presence to those who are alone, relief and resource support to loved ones and caregivers, and compassionate support through the last hours, allowing people to die in peace and with dignity. Anyone can join an existing chapter or start a new one in their area. Contact: Compassion in Action, P.O. Box 84013, Los Angeles, CA 90073; (213) 931-7315; Web site www.TwilightBrigade.com. To inquire about the hospice work of Nadia McCaffrey, write to her at 67 Robinhood Drive, San Rafael, CA 94901-1460.

3. These two books are excellent sources to explore: Mary Ann Block, D.O., *No More Ritalin* (New York: Kensington, 1996); Judith Ullman, *Ritalin Free Kids: Safe and Effective Homeopathic Medicine for ADD and Other Behavior and Learning Problems* (Rockland, Calif.: Prima, 1996).

4. Diane K. Corcoran, R.N., Ph.D., regularly travels across the nation and through other countries teaching thousands of

nurses and health-care providers about their role in support-
ing patients who have had a near-death experience. As a two-
term past president of the International Association for
Near-Death Studies, she has been privy to the latest in
research and information on experiencer needs. As another
adjunct to her work, she has teamed up with Maggie
Callanan, R.N., a hospice nurse and coauthor of the book
*Final Gifts: Understanding the Special Awareness, Needs, and
Communications of the Dying* (with Patricia Kelley; New York:
Simon & Schuster, 1992). Together, these two dynamic
speakers offer Shades of the Rainbow, a full-day workshop on
near-death states and nearing-death awareness, to any group
willing to sponsor them. To discuss this further, contact Dr.
Corcoran at 10705 Oldfield, Reston, VA 22091; (703) 922-
5562; fax (703) 476-1553.

5. The entire story of Cheryl Pottberg's amazing recovery and Dr.
Gerald M. Lemole's equally amazing conversion to holistic
health measures is chronicled as a front-page feature article in
the Life & Leisure section of the (Wilmington, Delaware) *Sunday
News Journal* (July 13, 1997, section J). Contact Dr. Lemole
through his office at the Medical Arts Pavilion, Suite 205, 4745
Ogletown Road, Newark, DE 19713-2070; (302) 738-0448. His
title is Chief of Cardiovascular Surgery, and his training and credentials are impeccable. Teaming up with two other surgeons,
he has established the M.D.'s Medical Healthline at (900) GET-
WELL ($1.99 per minute) to provide recorded information on
more than fifty diseases and problems, and to give "the truth
about natural remedies." Anyone can avail him- or herself of this
service. The average call lasts about five minutes.

6. Betty Eadie, *Embraced by the Light* (Placerville, Calif.: Gold Leaf
Press, 1992).

Six: Many Types, One Pattern

1. The purpose as stated on Timothy O'Reilly's forty-minute
video *Round Trip* is to "educate, enlighten, and heal." To obtain
a copy, order from Wellspring Media, 65 Bleecker Street, New
York, NY 10012; (800) 538-5856.

2. Amanda Csanady, then seven, did the drawing for the month of June in the 1987–1988 Mead Johnson Enfamil Calendar, published by Mead Johnson Nutritionals, 2400 West Expressway, Evansville, IN 47721-0001; (812) 429-5000. My thanks to Mead Johnson for allowing me to use Amanda's winning entry.

3. I wrote extensively about correlations of significance between the color yellow and the chemistry of the brain in *Beyond the Light* (pages 180–182 in the paperback version). A further discussion can be found in my research report *Brain Shift/Spirit Shift: A Theoretical Model Using Research on Near-Death States to Explore the Transformation of Consciousness.* The report can be obtained through my Web site at www.cinemind.com/atwater or from me directly at You Can Change Your Life, P.O. Box 7691, Charlottesville, VA 22906-7691. Send a stamped, self-addressed envelope for a reply, or access the Web site.

4. "Students' Post Near-Death Experience Attitude and Behavior Toward Education and Learning," a Ph.D. dissertation by Joseph Benedict Geraci, is on file at the University of Connecticut, Storrs, Connecticut.

5. I discuss the issue of therapy and memory recall in "Tips for the 'Child' in All of Us," one of three "missing" appendixes to this book. Because of space limitations, it was necessary for me to put this and the other two appendixes on my Web site. They are also available from me directly as a separate text. Access my Web site at www.cinemind.com/atwater, or contact me through You Can Change Your Life, P.O. Box 7691, Charlottesville, VA 22906-7691. Send a stamped, self-addressed envelope for information. For information on my Web site, see pages 235–236.

Seven: Cases from History

1. For more information about Lincoln, see: L. Pierce Clark, *Lincoln: A Psycho-Biography* (New York: Charles Scribner's Sons, 1933). Ida M. Tarbell, *The Early Life of A.L.* (New

Brunswick, N.J.: A. S. Barnes and Co., 1974). Emanuel Hertz, *The Hidden Lincoln, from the Letters and Papers of Wm. H. Herndon* (New York: Viking Press, 1938). Joseph E. Suppiger, *The Intimate Lincoln* (Lanham, Md.: University Press of America, 1985). Ward H. Lamon, *The Life of A. Lincoln, from His Birth to His Inauguration as President* (Boston: James R. Osgood & Co., 1872). Richard N. Current, *The Lincoln Nobody Knows* (New York: McGraw Hill, 1958).

2. Refer to John Neihardt, *Black Elk Speaks* (New York: Pocket Books, 1972). Also obtain audiocassette #SU-6 from the 1995 IANDS conference on the near-death phenomenon. This is a tape of a talk by Steve Straight on the connection between Black Elk and his biographer, John Neihardt: *both had had childhood near-death experiences and understood each other perfectly.* The tape is still available and can be ordered from: IANDS, P.O. Box 502, East Windsor Hill, CT 06028-0502; (860) 644-5216; Web site www.iands.org.

3. Walter and Lao Russell have long since passed on, but their University of Science and Philosophy is still active, although currently undergoing restructuring. Their home-study correspondence course, all their books, plus Glenn Clark's biography of Walter Russell, titled *The Man Who Tapped the Secrets of the Universe,* are available to anyone interested. Contact: University of Science and Philosophy, P.O. Box 520, Waynesboro, VA 22980; (800) 882-LOVE or (540) 942-5161; fax (540) 942-8705; Web site www.philosophy.org. Query about the video tour of the Russells' home.

4. *Infinite Mind: Science of the Human Vibrations of Consciousness* is a 1996 version of Valerie V. Hunt's original book, *Infinite Mind: The Science of Human Vibrations* (Malibu, Calif.: Malibu Publishing Co., 1989). Little changed between the two editions except for the title and a few corrections. Contact: Malibu Publishing Co., P.O. Box 4234, Malibu, CA 90265. Many of Hunt's music and sound audiocassette tapes are also available, as is a video on the human energy field. (Details in

the back of her book or through the publisher.) My thanks to Dr. Hunt for the right to quote from her material.

5. Inquire about newsletter subscriptions by contacting Raymond A. Moody, Jr., M.D., Ph.D., at Theater of the Mind, P.O. Box 417, Anniston, AL 36202; (205) 831-0199; fax (205) 831-9889. Be alert for Moody's latest book, *The Last Laugh* (Charlottesville, Va.: Hampton Roads Publishing, 1999). His Web site address is: www.lifeafterlife.com/body_index.html.

Eight: Evidence for a Life Continuum

1. In the paperback edition of *Beyond the Light* (Avon Books, 1997), I discussed the case of Berkley Carter Mills as an example of the Transcendent Experience. The quote that appears here is from page 73 of the paperback and is used with his kind permission.

2. The Pleasant and/or Heaven-like Experience of Alice Morrison-Mays appears on pages 56–60 of the paperback edition of *Beyond the Light* (Avon Books). My thanks to Alice for giving me the right to reuse some of her material and for permission to quote from her additional comments.

3. Arvin S. Gibson, "Near-Death Experience Patterns from Research in the Salt Lake City Region," *Journal of Near-Death Studies* 13, no. 2 (Winter 1994). The specific quote used appears on page 125. Gibson wrote a series of three books, each a collection of accounts from the near-death survivors he interviewed. These are: *Glimpses of Eternity* (1992), *Echoes from Eternity* (1993), and *Journeys Beyond Life* (1994), all published by Horizon Publishers in Bountiful, Utah.

4. Robert L. Van de Castle, Ph.D., *Our Dreaming Mind: A Sweeping Exploration of the Role That Dreams Have Played in Politics, Art, Religion, and Psychology, from Ancient Civilizations to the Present Day* (New York: Ballantine Books, 1994).

5. Caryl Dennis, with Parker Whitman, *The Millennium Children: Tales of the Shift*. Dennis self-published this book in 1997. The book is available through: Rainbows Unlimited,

1245 Palm Street, Clearwater, FL 34615; (813) 441-2270. Prepare yourself, for the book is printed on lavender-colored paper. The section about vanishing twins is on pages 138–166.

6. Raymond W. Brandt, Ph.D., publishes both *Twins World* magazine and *Twinless Twins* newsletter. To obtain these publications plus information about annual conferences, contact: Twinless Twins Support International, 11220 St. Joe Road, Fort Wayne, IN 46835; (219) 627-5414.

7. The research bulletin "Multiple Personality—Mirrors of a New Model of Mind?" vol. 1, no. 3/4, is a double issue and is available from: Institute of Noetic Sciences, 475 Gate Five Road, Suite 300, Sausalito, CA 94965; (415) 331-5650.

8. *Newsweek* magazine, special edition, "From Birth to Three" (Spring/Summer 1997). The quote is from Geoffrey Cowley's article, "The Language Explosion," on page 17.

9. Thomas Verny, M.D., with John Kelly, *The Secret Life of the Unborn Child* (New York: Dell, 1981).

10. David Chamberlain, Ph.D., *Babies Remember Birth* (Los Angeles: Jeremy Tarcher, 1988).

11. David B. Cheek, M.D., "Are Telepathy, Clairvoyance, and 'Hearing' Possible in Utero? Suggestive Evidence as Revealed During Hypnotic Age-Regression," *Journal of Pre- & Peri-Natal Psychology* 7, issue 2 (Winter 1992): 125–137.

12. Ian Stevenson, M.D., *Twenty Cases Suggestive of Reincarnation* (New York: American Society for Psychical Research, 1966), and *Where Reincarnation and Biology Intersect* (Glenview, Ill.: Praeger, 1997).

13. Carol Bowman, *Children's Past Lives: How Past Life Memories Affect Your Child* (New York: Bantam, 1997).

14. Two leaders in the field of NDA (nearing-death awareness) are Maggie Callanan and Patricia Kelley. Their book is *Final Gifts: Understanding the Special Awareness, Needs, and Communication of the Dying* (New York: Simon & Schuster, 1992).

15. Two pioneers in ADC (after-death communication) are Bill Guggenheim and Judy Guggenheim, authors of *Hello from*

Heaven: A New Field of Research Confirms That Life and Love Are Eternal (New York: Bantam Books, 1996). Contact them directly if you wish to report an ADC or participate in their research: The ADC Project, P.O. Box 916070, Longwood, FL 32791; (407) 862-1260.

16. Works by those spearheading research into PBEs (prebirth experiences) are: Sarah Hinze, *Coming from the Light: Spiritual Accounts of Life Before Birth* (New York: Pocket Books, 1994). Hinze is actively seeking more accounts of the PBE. Contact her through: Royal Child Studies, P.O. Box 31086, Mesa, AZ 85275-1086; (602) 898-3009. Craig Lundahl and Harold Widdison, *The Eternal Journey: How Near-Death Experiences Illuminate Our Earthly Lives* (New York: Warner Books, 1997). Elisabeth Hallett, *Soul Trek: A Pioneering Study of Pre-Birth Communications* (Hamilton, Mont.: Light Hearts Publishing, 1995).

Nine: Alien Existences

1. An intriguing collection of stories about the missing fetus syndrome is found in Jenny Randles, *Star Children: The True Story of Alien Offspring Among Us* (New York: Sterling Publishing Co., 1995). *Caution:* Randles's list of characteristics that she says distinguish "star children" is *exactly the same as the list that identifies average, typical child experiencers of near-death states.* There is reason to question this "coincidence" and wonder what differences would emerge if research between the phenomena were compared in a more thorough and careful manner. The fact that a child fits Randles's list *does not mean he or she is "alien."*

2. Ben Okri, *The Famished Road* (New York: Anchor Books, 1993). My thanks to Doubleday for their generous permission in allowing me to quote from Okri's work. My thanks also to Donald Riggs of Thorigne Sur Due, France, for recommending Okri to me. Okri writes from a child's perspective of modern Nigeria that is most extraordinary, and creates striking word pictures.

3. Flavio M. Cabobianco, *Vengo del Sol (I Come from the Sun)* (Buenos Aires, Argentina: Organizacion Zago S.R.L., 1991). French and German translations are available; an English version should be out in 1999. I want to thank Flavio and Marcos Cabobianco for their many kindnesses, and Alejandra Warden for translating our conversation and Flavio's book. Thanks also go to Florin Lowndes for bringing along a German copy of Flavio's book when he stayed in our home. What I saw as he translated each page convinced me that I had to locate the Cabobianco family, and I did so with the help of Stephany Evans.

4. Peter Graneau, "Is Dead Matter Aware of Its Environment?" *Frontier Perspectives* 7, no. 1 (Fall/Winter 1998): 50–52. If you encounter any difficulty locating this journal, contact: Center for Frontier Sciences, Temple University, Ritter Hall, Room 478, 1301 Cecil B. Moore Avenue, Philadelphia, PA 19122; (215) 204-8487.

5. Kenneth Ring, Ph.D., *The Omega Project: Near-Death Experiences, UFO Encounters, and Mind at Large* (New York: William Morrow, 1992).

6. Greta Woodrew, LL.D., and her husband, Dick Smolowe, LL.D., were publishers of the newsletter *Woodrew Update* until the fall of 1997, when they retired the periodical after seventeen years of "holding forth." Copies of volume 17, number 3 are still available, as are other past issues, Woodrew's books *On a Slide of Light* and *Memories of Tomorrow,* and her coloring book for children, titled *Hear the Colors! See the Music!* Contact: Woodrew and Smolowe, Star Cove, 5450 Bermuda Village, Advance, NC 27006; (910) 940-2339; e-mail STARFDN@PRODIGY.NET

7. Ruth Montgomery, *Strangers Among Us* (New York: Coward, McCann, Geoghegan, 1979).

8. Proponents of the walk-in theory, or "soul switching," have formed an organization that sponsors regular conferences. Contact: WE International, P.O. Box 120633, St. Paul, MN 55112; e-mail WalkinsLiz@aol.com

Ten: A New Race Aborning

1. Refer back to note 1 in chapter 1.
2. This is an old Sumerian legend sculpted in relief on actual dated artifacts, thought to be symbolic by most archaeologists, but taken as factual by researcher Zecharia Sitchen in many of his books. Refer to Zecharia Sitchen, *Genesis Revisited: Is Modern Science Catching Up with Ancient Knowledge?* (Santa Fe, N.M.: Bear & Co., 1990).
3. For more than forty years Edgar Cayce would close his eyes, enter an altered state of consciousness, and speak to the very heart and spirit of humankind on subjects such as health, dreams, prophecy, meditation, and reincarnation. Dubbed the "sleeping prophet," he has since passed on, but his work continues through the Association for Research and Enlightenment (A.R.E.), P.O. Box 595, Virginia Beach, VA 23451; general information is available at (800) 333-4499; the bookstore phone number is (888) ARE-0050. Anyone can visit their extensive library. Membership is yearly; they offer a wide range of services and products and have active study groups of the Cayce material worldwide.
4. One interpretation of this is found in Kirk Nelson, *The Second Coming* (Virginia Beach, Va.: Wright Publishing Co., 1986).
5. An excellent reference for the legend of the White Buffalo is Robert B. Pickering, *Seeing the White Buffalo* (Denver, Colo: Denver Museum of Natural History Press, 1997).
6. Gordon-Michael Scallion, *Notes from the Cosmos: A Futurist's Insights into the World of Dream Prophecy and Intuition—Includes Global Predictions for 1998–2012.* Originally published by his company in 1997, it should be available in any bookstore. If not, contact: Matrix Institute, Inc., P.O. Box 367, West Chesterfield, N.H. 03466-0367; (603) 256-6520; fax (603) 256-6614; Web site www.matrixinstitute.com. Scallion publishes the monthly *Earth Changes Report* and a large map of what his visions have shown him that the world will be like after "the changes." All quotes are used with his kind permission.
7. Swami Amritasvarupananda, *Mata Amritanandamayi: A Biography*

(San Ramon, Calif.: Mata Amritanandamayi Center, 1988). This book should be available through any bookstore. Or, order from: Mata Amritanandamayi Center, P.O. Box 613, San Ramon, CA 94583-0613; (510) 537-9417; fax (510) 889-8585; Web site www.ammachi.org. Quotes are excerpted from pages 14–16 and 193. I want to thank Swami Paramatmananda for giving me permission to use the quotes, and Helen Williams of Vancouver, British Columbia, for telling me about Mata Amritanandamayi.

8. John White has written fifteen books, which have been translated into nine languages; among them is the classic *The Meeting of Science and Spirit* (New York: Paragon House, 1990).

9. Refer back to chapter 1, note 1. The quote carried here can be found on page 341 of Strauss and Howe's *Generations.*

10. E. Alan Meece, *Horoscope for the New Millennium* (St. Paul, Minn.: Llewellyn, 1997). Meece excerpted parts of his book for the article "The Generations: An Overview," which was carried in the May/June 1997 issue of *Welcome to Planet Earth* magazine. Contact: The Great Bear, P.O. Box 12007, Eugene, OR 97440; (541) 683-1760. This magazine, by the way, is an outstanding source for well-researched articles about astrology and its influence on society and politics.

11. The Adawee Teachings are produced as part of the Honor Series of Entertainment/Educational Tools. For more information, contact: Linda Redford, 1034 Ninth Street, Apt. 9, Santa Monica, CA 90403; (310) 392-1200; Web site www .honorkids.com.

Eleven: The Promise

1. For more information about Paul Ray's categorization of "cultural creatives," refer to Cathy Madison, "Reality Hunger," *Utne Reader,* July/August 1997, 55.

2. Charlene Spretnak, *The Resurgence of the Real: Body, Nature, and Place in a Hypermodern World* (Reading, Mass.: Addison-Wesley, 1997).

3. Third-way principles are discussed in chapter 20 of *Future*

Memory (New York: Birch Lane Press, 1996; Charlottesville, Va.: Hampton Roads Publishing Co., 1999). Also, see chapter 3 in John Nelson, ed., *Solstice Shift: Magical Blend's Synergistic Guide to the Coming Age* (Charlottesville, Va.: Hampton Roads Publishing Co., 1997). I penned both chapters.

4. Walter Starcke, *It's All God* (Boerne, Tex.: Guadalupe Press, 1998). Should you have any difficulty obtaining this book, or want to avail yourself of Starcke's past works, contact: Guadalupe Press, P.O. Box 865, Boerne, TX 78006; (830) 537-4655; e-mail starcke@gvtc.com. I want to thank Walter Starcke for his kind permission in allowing me to quote him.

5. The most documented of weather-pattern study and human-behavior links is James DeMeo, *Saharasia: The 4000 BCE Origins of Child Abuse, Sex-Repression, Warfare and Social Violence in the Deserts of the Old World* (Greensprings, Ore.: Orgone Biophysical Research Lab, 1998). If you are unable to locate this book, contact: Orgone Biophysical Research Lab, Inc., Greensprings Center, P.O. Box 1148, Ashland, OR 97520; (541) 552-0118; e-mail demeo@mind.net.

6. Refer to Jeremy Rifkin, *The Biotech Century* (New York: Tarcher/Putnam, 1998).

7. New Visions for Child Care, Inc., focuses on preschool and after-school learning opportunities, as well as functioning as an umbrella for New Global Visions for Children's Television. Muriel Freifeld's mission is to tailor learning programs to meet children's individual needs. "It's the kids who tell me what they need," she explained, "not someone's theory." To avail yourself of her expertise or to inquire about her innovative programs, write to her at 10737 Deborah Drive, Potomac, MD 20854.

8. Refer specifically to the work of Rupert Sheldrake in his books, *A New Science of Life: The Hypothesis of Formative Causation* (Los Angeles: Tarcher, 1981), and *The Presence of the Past: Morphic Resonance and the Habits of Nature* (New York: Times Books, 1989).

9. Ken Wilber, *The Spectrum of Consciousness* (Wheaton, Ill.: Theosophy Publishing House, 1993). This is the twentieth-anniversary edition.

10. Mark Matousek, "Up Close and Transpersonal with Ken Wilber," *Utne Reader,* July/August 1998, 50–55, 106–107.
11. Ken Wilber, *The Marriage of Sense and Soul: Integrating Science and Religion* (New York: Random House, 1998).
12. Ursula King, *Spirit of Fire: The Life and Vision of Teilhard de Chardin* (Maryknoll, N.Y.: Orbis Books, 1996).

I am brilliant. I am golden. I am a starchild of God. I illumine my world with the light of the highest heaven.

The Reverend Coco Stewart

Grateful acknowledgment is made to the following for permission to reprint from the following material:

Solara J'an Blessing: "Fly" by Solara J'an Blessing. Reprinted by permission of the author.

Doubleday, a division of Random House, Inc.: excerpt from *The Famished Road* by Ben Okri. Copyright © 1993 by Anchor Books. Reprinted by permission of Doubleday, a division of Random House, Inc.

Joseph Benedict Geraci: excerpt from previously unpublished work for his Ph.D. dissertation, "Students' Post Near-Death Experience Attitude and Behavior Toward Education and Learning," on file at the University of Connecticut at Stoors. Reprinted by permission of the author.

Guadalupe Press: excerpt from *It's All God* by Walter Starcke. Copyright © 1998 by Guadalupe Press. Reprinted by permission of the author.

Hampton Roads Publishing Company, Inc.: excerpt from *Solstice Shift: Magical Blend's Synergistic Guide to the Coming Age,* edited by John Nelson. Copyright © 1999 by Hampton Roads Publishing Company, Inc. Reprinted by permission of Hampton Roads Publishing Company, Inc.

Dr. Valerie Hunt: excerpt from *Infinite Mind: Science of the Human Vibrations of Consciousness* by Dr. Valerie Hunt (Malibu Publishing Company). Copyright © 1996 by Malibu Publishing Company. Reprinted by permission of the author.

Mata Amritanandamayi Center: excerpt from *Mata Amritanandamayi: A Biography.* Copyright © 1988 by Mata Amritanandamayi Center. Reprinted by permission of M. A. Center.

The Matrix Institute: excerpt from *Notes from the Cosmos: A Futurist's Insights into the World of Dream and Prophecy and Intuition—Includes Global Prediction for 1998–2012* by Gordon-Michael Scallion. Copyright © 1997 by Matrix Institute. Reprinted by permission of the Matrix Institute.

Todd Murphy: excerpt from previously unpublished work, "The Structure and Function of Near-Death Experiences: An Algorithmic Hypothesis." Reprinted by permission of the author.

Rainbows Unlimited: excerpt from *The Millennium Children: Tales of the Shift* by Caryl Dennis. Copyright © 1997 by Rainbows Unlimited. Reprinted by permission of Rainbows Unlimited.

Linda Redford: the Honor Pledge and Honor Code from The Adawee Teachings. Reprinted by permission of the author.

Woodrew Update Newsletter: excerpt from *Woodrew Update,* vol. 17, no. 3. Reprinted by permission of Greta Woodrew, Ph.D.

INDEX

Index

ABOUT THE AUTHOR

P. M. H. ATWATER is one of the original researchers of the near-death phenomenon, having begun her work in 1978. Today, her contribution to the field of near-death studies is considered on par with those of Raymond Moody and Kenneth Ring. Her first two books, *Coming Back to Life* and *Beyond the Light,* are considered the bibles of the near-death experience. With the publication of *Future Memory,* she has expanded her work into areas of brain development that call for a reconsideration of what is presently known about transformations of consciousness. Rune casting with the elder yin or Goddess Runes became therapy for her after she survived three death events that produced three different near-death experiences in 1977. Her investigation of these primordial runic glyphs led to her book *Goddess Runes,* offered as thanks for what she has gained and also to pass on the skill of rune casting. *Children of the New Millennium* promises to be her most provocative work yet.